To Trish,

Here's to all your greatest aspirations now fulfilled!

All my love!

Uchechi Gpike-Bosse

From Aspiration to Fulfillment

Bridging the gap from where you are to where you want to be

Uchechi Ezurike-Bosse

BALBOA.
PRESS
A DIVISION OF HAY HOUSE

Balboa Press books may be ordered through booksellers or by contacting:

Balboa Press
A Division of Hay House
1663 Liberty Drive
Bloomington, IN 47403
www.balboapress.com
1 (877) 407-4847

Because of the dynamic nature of the Internet, any web addresses or links contained in this book may have changed since publication and may no longer be valid. The views expressed in this work are solely those of the author and do not necessarily reflect the views of the publisher, and the publisher hereby disclaims any responsibility for them.

The author of this book does not dispense medical advice or prescribe the use of any technique as a form of treatment for physical, emotional, or medical problems without the advice of a physician, either directly or indirectly. The intent of the author is only to offer information of a general nature to help you in your quest for emotional and spiritual well-being. In the event you use any of the information in this book for yourself, which is your constitutional right, the author and the publisher assume no responsibility for your actions.

Any people depicted in stock imagery provided by Thinkstock are models, and such images are being used for illustrative purposes only.
Certain stock imagery © Thinkstock.

Print information available on the last page.

ISBN: 978-1-5043-7141-4 (sc)
ISBN: 978-1-5043-7143-8 (hc)
ISBN: 978-1-5043-7142-1 (e)

Library of Congress Control Number: 2016920602

Balboa Press rev. date: 01/05/2017

Contents

Introduction

Why I'm Writing this Book

This book you now hold in your hands has been a dream of mine for a very long time. It was born from my thirst to have more passion and purpose in my life, to know exactly how I could change my circumstances and become a deliberate creator of my life and fulfill all my greatest aspirations.

I've always had an insatiable quench to create more joy and freedom in my life. I wanted to feel fulfilled, happy and live life on my terms. For the longest time, I've felt so out of control and frustrated that I haven't been able to impact my life the way I wanted too. I read the books, watched the DVDs, attended seminars, webinars, you name it and have been inspired by so many great teachers.

One thing that stood out for me is that many teachers taught the same message over and over again. The style and format in which they shared may differ, but at the end of the day the message was always the same.

I never got tired of learning and hearing the messages from different perspectives. I used to wonder how my perspective would give new meaning and what new lessons I could offer. But I now realize that my perspective may give you some value, because my experience and viewpoint may resonate with you differently than others. This has happened to me in the past. I'd hear the same message from different teachers, yet one connected with me more through the way they expressed it. Their personal stories and style allowed their message to sink in, and it was then that I was able to apply it to my life and stir me into action. That is my wish for you, as you go through this book; that you awaken to the possibilities that are available to you.

You have the ability to co-create your life and live consciously instead of being driven by unconscious programming and past limiting beliefs that keep you from reaching your greatest desires. I'm here to tell you that yes, indeed, your desires and aspirations *can* and *will* be fulfilled. There is a process, and one that only you can decide to embark on. It's a simple process, not necessarily an easy one, but I promise it'll be well worth it to understand how to bridge the gap to your dreams!

I hope that as you read this book, you take action. I'll talk more about action later, but know that one of the biggest differences between those that actually realize their dreams and those that don't, comes down to action. The former took consistent action no matter how small or uncomfortable it might have been. They understand that action is crucial to the fulfillment of their dreams.

If you desire to experience more joy and have big dreams, remember that you, yes *you*, hold the key to unlocking your potential. All the resources you need to make it happen are all within your reach.

If this message resonates with you, then you know

there's a deeper part of you, recognizing this truth, the truth that you can indeed create an incredible life, and achieve your greatest desires. It's time to go from aspiring to actually *fulfilling* your dreams.

CHAPTER 1

Your Current Conditions

"The greatest act of courage is to be and to own all of who you are – without apology, without excuses, without masks to cover the truth of who you are."
~ Debbie Ford

If you're reading this book, then it's a safe bet that there's an area of your life you want to improve, or a goal you want to achieve. It could be to have a committed and loving relationship, or sharing your gifts through business ownership or having freedom to travel the world. It doesn't matter what the form of your desire is, chances are you have it.

The truth is, we *all* have this need. It's a human condition to want more and to live the fullest expression of ourselves. It's our soul yearning to be fully expressed. My beloved teacher, the late Dr. Wayne Dyer, used to sing the song "Don't fence me in" when he used to speak on stage, to refer to how the soul longs to be expressed. Our soul wants to be set free and to fully express itself, because being confined goes against our soul's purpose.

To live fully and freely may be a hard concept to grasp because many of us have lived our lives being confined. We've been conditioned to limit ourselves to what we can have, be and do. We've held ourselves back in so many ways. It seems like only a limited number of people actually feel free to live the life they want.

In order to take you on the journey of getting from where you are to where you want to be, I want you to first start by taking inventory of your current circumstances. I believe in order to head to a new destination, it's important to first identify your starting point.

Whatever you're experiencing in this moment has been a result of your past thoughts, beliefs and actions. I know this is not the first time you've heard this, nor will it be the last time, because it's the ultimate truth. Anything that you have in your life has been manifested by you whether consciously or- often times- unconsciously.

If you feel you have little control, and your outside world is controlling your life, let this be your wake-up call. It's time to take responsibility. What's great about this is that regardless of what is happening around you, you have the ability to transcend it. It means you don't have to wait or depend on anybody or any circumstance outside of you to change. It means you can take back control and do what's needed in order to transform your life.

You might be asking how it is you've manifested your current conditions. How is it you got to where you're now sitting?

Your current conditions are nothing but a projection of past thoughts, feelings and actions. They are memories of your past showing up in physical manifestation.

Here's the thing, you are always and forever creating. You're a manifesting machine and most times operate on autopilot. This autopilot is your subconscious mind. It's in the driver's seat controlling your environment, based on your thoughts and beliefs.

Look at your habitual thoughts, words and beliefs about your life. Do you believe that life is a struggle? Maybe you have a deep belief that money is hard to get and you're not worthy of it. How about the belief that you can't make a living doing what you love? These are the types of beliefs many people have that hold them back. This was the case for me. I had a big belief that being rich was not safe and because of this, I struggled to make ends meet.

I always feared having large amounts of cash in my wallet or at home. I would get really nervous in the possession of large bills; it just did not feel safe. If I had to pay cash for something and a large amount, the act of handing out large bills scared me. I feared someone seeing the large amount of money would want to rob or hurt me in some way to get it.

This subconscious fear limited the amount of wealth I allowed myself to have. Anything above a certain threshold, I would unconsciously resist. It was work and still is, for me to clear this belief and instil new empowering ones.

To identify the limiting beliefs you hold, it's good to look back to your childhood as a starting point. It is said that before the age of six or seven, the majority of your beliefs were formed. I first learnt this through the teachings of Bob Proctor. Before the age of seven, whatever we heard and experienced was dropped into our subconscious mind. Our mind was an open vessel and we did not have the conscious awareness to refute anything that was implanted in it.

Whatever we observed in our environment was impressed directly into our subconscious mind and became our beliefs. Those formative years have been described as a type of hypnosis. When we watched and observed the actions of our parents and those in authority, those behaviours dropped straight into our subconscious mind.

I recently read an interview with Dr. Bruce Lipton, a stem cell biologist, bestselling author and international speaker. Dr. Lipton in the interview stated that psychologists believe that 70% of the conditioning downloaded before the age of seven was limiting beliefs that are self-sabotaging and disempowering. These beliefs hold you back and do not support your dreams and desires. No wonder many people struggle to achieve their goals!

So, if you grew up in a household where your parents struggled for money and found it difficult to achieve success and they openly expressed it through their words, then that information dropped down to you. With repetition and emotion, you took on those same beliefs.

This is the same as 'stories' you may have written about yourself. If you were told you weren't smart enough or pretty enough and that people like you can't do something, then that became the story you wrote about yourself and life.

Whatever area you may be struggling in, it is nothing but a result of some long-held beliefs about yourself.

A lot of people have been conditioned to believe that they are neither good enough nor worthy and that becomes the lens from which they see their world. From that perspective you'll see things that prove your thoughts to be true, thus reinforcing your beliefs.

If you've created conditions you don't want, then see this as an opportunity for healing and growth. When you see it from this perspective you come from an empowered place versus feeling like a victim to your circumstance. Welcome it as a chance to heal past errors in the thinking that led you here.

Cycle of Reality

I want to share something I first came across when I was doing my life coaching certification. I trained under Master Life Coach Mark Fournier through his program *Life Mastery ~ A Course of Action*. In this course, I was introduced to a concept that explains why and how we see the reality we perceive.

The cycle of reality starts with your *focus*. This focus can be conscious or unconscious. As you'll learn in more detail in this book, everything you focus on expands and you'll see and experience more of the same things in your life. More than likely your biggest focus has been on areas of your life that you'd like to change and things that appear to not be working for you.

The next step Mark teaches is your *self-talk*, which is formed based on what you've been focusing on. Self-talk is nothing more than your habitual thoughts that constantly go on in your head. When your self talk is focused on a particular area, you give it power to create more of the same whether your self-talk and focus is good or bad.

Your self-talk then begins to take on a life of its own and turns into a *story* you create about how life is. The fleeting thoughts of 'Oh my, I have a hard time balancing my books', becomes a story of how "Even if I make money, I'll lose it because I suck at handling money!" With every thought you have regarding the situation, you build on it and it becomes stronger.

Once you've convinced yourself of the story and you buy into it, it then becomes the *reality* that you perceive. Your belief in the story is so real despite any evidence to the contrary.

Once your story is in place, it then affects the way you *feel*. Going back to the example of how you're unable to balance your books because you suck at handling money, you begin to feel badly about money and the lack of it in your life, convinced that there is no way you can ever get past it and have more than enough to live on!

Your feelings then affect the way you *behave*. Mark's famous for saying; 'we behave appropriately to the way we feel.' So you begin to hoard money and possible try to haggle your way into getting discounts and paying less and not even looking at another possibility for increasing your income. Your awareness, feeling and energy is on lack and as a result you behave accordingly.

The final cycle of reality Mark teaches is *evidence*. Because you're the cause of what you see based on your thoughts and feelings, your outer world reflects it back to you. You create evidence that supports your focus, self-talk, stories, reality, feeling and behaviour, and the cycle starts all over again. As you haggle your way to get deals and hoard, you then create more circumstances where you feel the need to continue to hoard and not have enough. As a result, it confirms your perceived reality that there's never enough money, you feel stuck and again your focus is on lack.

I'd like to share an example that I've seen in my own life that illustrates this. I grew up in a single parent home and it was always my mom and two sisters. The majority of the friends I grew up with were also raised in a single mother household. As a result, my focus and belief was on the unavailability of men, because I did not see them in my life growing up.

I created the story of how men were never around and being in a so-called 'traditional' household was not the norm. My friends and I would say how 'there are no good men out there'. Consequently, this became my reality, as I was single most of my adulthood, thus reinforcing my belief of men being unavailable.

I remember feeling so frustrated at being single and wanting to meet someone who would feel the same about me as I did about them. Going out in the hopes of meeting someone almost felt like a waste of time because I felt I was not meeting the 'right one'. So I behaved appropriately to my feeling by resisting going out and meeting new people. As a result of my behaviour, I was not able to meet someone, thus again providing 'evidence' of my story of men not being available.

The ironic part was that on the day that I decided to go out with my sisters and some friends, even though I didn't feel like it and almost did not go out, was when I met the man who is now my husband. I would have missed out on him and our beautiful family had I remained stuck in my story.

Acknowledge and accept your current conditions

You now have a better idea of how it is you've manifested the conditions you presently face. In order to get to where you truly desire, it's important to first acknowledge *and* accept your current conditions. Take inventory of your current beliefs that have led you here.

Some people may find this difficult to do because they don't want to look at their 'shadows', but it's in looking at them and shining the light that those shadows can disappear.

A great exercise to do is to grab a piece of paper and a pen and start journaling. Write out what you feel your current conditions are and how you feel about it. Write things that you feel good about and things you'd like to change. The writing is not meant for you to obsess over things that may not be working for you, but rather a way to take inventory of your current conditions. If you're in debt, then find out the total amount and write it down. Please do not judge nor condemn yourself as you do this exercise. It's simply to bring into awareness your starting-point and areas of opportunity.

When doing this exercise, do it from a place of excitement, knowing that it's being written in order for transformation to occur. You are writing it down to identify areas of opportunities that you can improve upon.

Remember everything that has happened in your past that was not aligned to your desire was preparing you to now receive my words. You didn't make any mistakes nor should you place any blame for not yet achieving what you want. That is just your ego speaking. Everything that has occurred has led you to this point: the point where you're now ready for massive transformation. You're now ready to commit to making your dreams a reality and manifesting your heart's desire. So this is not about blame nor guilt, but an exciting opportunity that now awaits you!

As you take inventory of your current conditions, start to pay attention to what you tend to focus on. Is your mind pre-occupied with the bills you have and conditions that you want changed, or do you focus and daydream about what you want? What shows up in your regular conversations? All of this is creating your current conditions. You may not think it's important, but it is!

Take note as well of the people you surround yourself with. Jim Rohn famously said "we're the average of the five people we spend the most time with." If those people are habitual complainers take note, because chances are you'll take that on. If they hold great visions for themselves and inspire you to reach beyond where you are, take note of that too! These people greatly influence who you can be.

Allowing your shadows to feel safe

Acknowledging areas of your life that you may not like is what brings it to the surface, and creates a safe environment for you to *feel* so you can let it go.

We're told many times to only focus on the positive and resist the negative. However, I believe this causes the negative feelings to be stronger, because you're giving more energy to it, thus impressing it further into your mind and not allowing it the opportunity to be expressed. You are repressing the feeling and as a result it remains inside of you and sooner or later will find another outlet for release. As the saying goes, 'whatever you resist persists'.

When you safely allow your negative feelings to come up, you give it the space it needs to express and diminish. This happened to me. I had feelings I kept repressing and I had an energy healer tell me to allow it to come up and express it. I oftentimes feared my physical safety, felt trapped and a loss of control. I hated feeling this way and would try to get it out of my mind.

The energy healer said something that was a big 'aha' for me. She said, when you affirm the positive (through affirmations) and the negative voice comes up and you keep fighting to shut it up with the positive affirmation it's almost like you confuse your subconscious mind. It overloads it. I'll be explaining the subconscious mind in more detail later, but it really is like a computer. You do not want to overload it and that was exactly what I was doing when I was fighting my negative emotions by throwing more positive affirmation to it.

She told me to simply let the feelings come and it will only last about 5 seconds and then it'll go away. Just like that. And it did. Now some people may have more difficulty doing this, but I found for me, the less I pushed and pressured the feeling, the less it fought back. It's similar to what Liz Gilbert wrote in her book Big Magic when she says; "It seems to me that the less I fight my fear, the less it fights back. If I can relax, fear relaxes, too."

Another example I've heard that paints a beautiful picture is to see that voice and feeling like your inner child. Because, like I said, most of the programming we have that keeps us stuck was impressed when we were children and now runs our lives. So, it's like the child expressing its fears and we're forcing it to shut up. If we can simply see that voice and fear as our inner child and give it the space to express its feelings, be heard and seen, it'll then feel safe enough to calm down and the feeling will then dissipate.

I know my fear of physical safety that I just mentioned, came as a result of a traumatic event I had as a child. At the age of six, my sisters and I were almost abducted by a close family member and that experience left a huge impact on me. I remember seeing that family member getting out of a car and about three other men came out with him, swiftly walking towards us. My mother immediately started to scream in fear, and one of my sisters ran off. Being only six, I was taken with my mother and my other sister, forced into a car and they attempted to drive off. My mother refusing to allow them to drive off had her foot out attempting to stop them.

Thank goodness my mother saw a lady that used to baby-sit for us, and called out to her to call the police. I don't remember a lot after that, other than being stuck and feeling trapped in the car and the energy of anxiety and fear all around me.

I strongly believe this event led to my mild case of Obsessive Compulsive Disorder (OCD), and abnormal sense of fear for my physical safety because I felt a profound sense of loss of control, fear and anxiety.

I still struggle with OCD, but I now let myself off the hook for sometimes feeling fearful when I shouldn't. I know this is my inner child's imprint and expression of fear due to the events of my past. It's the memory replaying itself, only now I'm an adult and not in the same situation. My work is not to shut off that voice, but give it space to feel heard, supported, and safe, so the energy can flow out of me.

The other thing about facing and voicing your fears is that you're able to see its falsehood. I know you've heard of the acronym for fear being False Evidence Appearing Real. Fear is fed when you blind yourself from seeing the truth in things. If you fully embrace your fears and allow it space to express itself, you'll see that it's just an illusion, which gives you confidence to move beyond it. I know when I look at the situation when I'm feeling fearful, I can see how unfounded it is. This allows me to feel more comfortable and safe. I'm reminded of an English proverb that says; "Fear knocked at the door, Faith answered and nobody was there." Be willing to uncover the fears and negative emotions that are holding you back.

CHAPTER 2

Owning your Power

"Your power to choose your direction of your life
allows you to reinvent yourself, to change your future,
and to powerfully influence the rest of creation."
~Stephen Covey

You've probably heard many spiritual teachers say and write about the power each and every one of us possesses. This is something many of us hear, but never truly grasp the power of this truth.

When I think about my power and *your* power to create your life by design, it truly amazes me. I do want to state here that creation is not something you do in isolation and by yourself and that there is Divine order and assistance to this process. Human power is not enough to orchestrate this beautiful thing called life. Our power comes from an infinite source, and it doesn't matter by which name you call it, just know that it exists.

Throughout this book, I will call this power God, Universe or Source. Please enter whatever term fits with your spiritual practice and do not get caught up on the term used. Same definition, different terms and to get caught up on the label only limits you and your ability to create the life you want. I will go into greater depth on this later in this book, but right now, just understand that you are a co-creator and have the most powerful force in the universe as your ally.

To remind you of your power I want to refer you to Marianne Williamson's famous quote, "Our deepest fear is not that we are inadequate. Our deepest fear is that we are powerful beyond measure." I love that she writes 'we are powerful beyond measure', because it shows just how limitless we are. There is neither a cap nor ceiling to what you can be, have or achieve. The only limit really is what you place on it.

No matter what limitations you currently face, the great news is that it can be changed. It starts to change with the conscious act of recognizing your current thinking and way of being and doing the work to let go of all that's not in alignment with what you want.

You truly can achieve the greatest vision for your life. History gives us all kinds of examples of people overcoming great circumstances to achieve incredible results. Take the famous story of J.K Rowling who we all know as the famous writer of the Harry Potter book series. It is estimated that, J.K Rowling's worth is about 1 billion dollars and the majority of that coming from the Harry Potter book and movie franchise.

Her story is a true 'rags to riches' where she went from welfare as a single mom to multi-million dollar status in 5 years. Her manuscript was rejected 12 times from publishing companies. She was advised to get a day job since she had little chance of making any money in children's books. Against all odds, J.K Rowling became the woman we all now know. Someone who most people would look at in admiration wishing to experience some level of success that she now enjoys.

I'm here to tell you that J.K Rowling is no different than you in your ability to go after your dreams and make it happen. Whether consciously or unconsciously all achievements are a result of focus, persistence, faith and belief in ones' dream. You also have the same abilities to deliberately create your life and fulfill your biggest aspirations.

Understand that you have more say over your life than you realize. You get to choose what shows up in your life and you choose based on the habitual thoughts and feelings you have.

The Universal Law of Cause and Effect states that for every cause, there is an effect, and for every effect and circumstance in your life, there is a cause for it. You are the cause of the effects you are seeing. This is how powerful you are in the creation process.

You may have called in things you're not happy with, but you also have the power to transform anything you don't want. You can have and be anything you want, but first you must accept and believe it. Yes, you may have tried in the past to change certain things in your life without success, but my goal through the pages of this book is to show you why past attempts may have failed you, and show you simple, yet powerful ways to bridge the gap to your desires.

The Truth of who you are

Just as you identified your current conditions, it's important to also identify your current beliefs about who you think you are, and what you can achieve. You may have heard of the term *self-concept*. It's defined as "a collection of beliefs about oneself." Generally, self-concept embodies the answer to "Who am I?" So let me ask you: "Who are you?" Put down this book and think about it for a second.

If you're like most people, you answered by saying your sex, occupation, martial status etc. Now these may be descriptions of the roles you take on, but it's not an accurate definition of who you truly are.

The truth is, you are a powerful and infinite being with the divine presence within you. This is something you may have heard before and may either align or go against your current beliefs, but please try to consider it for a moment. This means both you and I, have the same creative ability as the one supreme power, because that supreme power, that divine presence is also present *in* us.

Let me stop for a moment and ask how that statement made you feel? The fact that you have the same creative ability as the Source. Was there any part of you that felt some resistance to this? Was it something that felt good *(me)* to contemplate or did it scare you? Maybe you felt it was somehow sinful to have such a thought! I sure felt this way when I was first introduced to this concept.

I used to feel that God was somehow outside of me and a deity that I had to prove myself to in order to remain in his favour. A deity that judged me and condemned my sins.

It was only when I realized that God was love and I did not have to 'win' his love, did things shift for me. I admit, my past conditioning sometimes shows up and I sometimes feel I need to prove myself, but I am able to remind myself of the beautiful truth that I am worthy just as I am.

I was also someone that prayed to God to do things *for* me, rather than *through* me. This is huge and I really want you to understand the difference here. When I prayed to God to do things *for* me, my expectation was that he would somehow magically make things happen and do my deeds for me. However, when I realized that is happens *through* me, I realized I had a part to play. It had to come through me and involve me and I had to take some kind of action and an active role to make things happen.

Another reason I struggled with the concept of being one with God was that growing up I felt separate from God/Universe, and like I said before, I really feared God. However, the more I grew to understand that God was love and I was made up from the same love was incredibly freeing and powerful for me. I knew that no matter how hard life may have appeared and things that showed up for me that I feared, the fact that I have this amazing loving power at my side gave me the strength to navigate whatever showed up for me.

This power and strength that we have within us, comes from the ultimate source. The Supreme Intelligence of life! This is why I love a passage from the metaphysical book A Course in Miracles that reads: "If you knew who walks beside you on the way that you have chosen, fear would be impossible." I don't know about you, but reading that gave me great comfort. It teaches that you don't have to be fearful in your journey. You're never alone in this crazy thing called life, regardless of the path that you take. You have a powerful companion at your side, guiding and able to give you strength, whenever you call on it.

Another great way to look at it is seeing yourself as part of an ocean. You are not the whole ocean, but a wave of it. However, the wave even though not as big as the ocean, has the same composition and qualities of the full ocean. Wayne Dyer used to say, "If you cut a slice of an apple pie, is the slice still not the pie?" This is a great way to think about it. You have the spark of God/Universe energy with you, as your co-creator.

When you grasp the power of this truth, you're then able to alleviate the limited vision you hold of yourself. You're able to recognize that you're more than just your body and the limitations you've placed on yourself. It gives you the confidence to know you have the power to be and do your heart's desire. You'll understand that you're enough and worthy of your dreams regardless of what life has thrown at you, and any mistakes you may have made.

Whatever guilt, negative images or emotions you may have had of yourself, you can drop that now. This is your time to see that whatever so-called 'bad' choices you've made up to this point, whether consciously or unconsciously does not define you. You are much more than your past experiences. You are a powerful creation that can change your life and impact those around you. If only you accept this and live with this new understanding, you can truly transform your life.

You are enough, exactly as you are and are worthy of your dreams. No, you don't need to be smarter, thinner, and funnier to have what you want. You deserve to live your dream life and it is truly possible for you right at this very moment.

Like I mentioned previously, you have the amazing ability to manifest. Yes, you may have been trying to consciously manifest things in your life that felt like they're not showing up, but know that yes indeed you are a brilliant manifester. You've more than likely manifested your current conditions without even knowing it, meaning it was done without your conscious awareness, and based on your past programs and conditioning. Programs you've bought into and believed to be true, regardless of if they were positive or negative.

The great news is that the work you're doing now in reading this book is helping you recognize your current conditioning, and providing you tools to help you push past your old conditioning, to finally obtain the goals you want.

Something that many people do when it comes to creating change and transforming their lives, is that they feel they are separate from it. Remember, that in order to achieve your dreams, you do not need to do anything or 'get' anything. Everything you need is all *within* you. I know this sounds cliché, but it's true. The only thing you need to do is remove the veil that's blocking you from seeing who you truly are.

You need to own your power and align yourself with how you want to live your life. I love the acorn example people often give. The oak tree is not outside the acorn is it? The big beautiful oak tree resides within the acorn.

You plant the acorn and with the right condition (light, water etc.) the acorn transitions into an oak tree. Yes, it requires cracking of the shell and time, which is a beautiful metaphor for life as you will have to crack open and shed the identity that you now define yourself with in order to become the full version of yourself. However, this transformation is already inside of you ready to emerge. So everything you need for your miracle to occur really is already inside of you. With the right 'conditions' of your thoughts and beliefs, you'll also transition into your fullest expression.

Your Power to Choose

Regardless of what is happening in your world, you have the power to choose your life experiences right now. You hold the key to the transformation you want. The key to conscious creation comes from the choices you make. In the past you may have made choices on auto-pilot without giving much thought to it. Or like many people, you felt more re-active than proactive to the events around you.

The great thing about human beings is our ability to choose and decide what we want. Decision is the starting point to the movement of getting you what you want. When you make the decision you *must* commit to it no matter what! No more second-guessing yourself and your ability to make it happen. It is my deepest belief that if you have a desire within you, then simultaneously you have the ability to make it happen. If you did not, then the desire would not have been felt. If you feel and desire it, then you're indeed able to make it happen.

The book you now hold in your hands is a great example. There was a desire within me to share my message through a book and reach more people with teachings that have impacted my life in a profound way. I had no idea how to start. Yes, I've written blogs on my website and some small e-books/workbooks, but nothing to this magnitude. I did not know first where to start, what the topic would be, nor the structure and how to publish it.

Even though, I did not know where to begin, I held onto the vision of seeing my physical book and made the decision that it will happen. I even printed out a book cover with my picture and a title (which is not the title I ended up going with), and I put the cover over a book to be reminded of my goal and to imprint my mind that it is a done deal.

I was led to a way to self-publish, and started putting the outline together. There were delays in getting this book written as different priorities came up for me. However, when I focused and made the decision to get this book written no matter what, I was able to write and produce the work you now hold in your hands. This was a desire that was manifested into reality through commitment to my writing and a *decision* to see it to completion.

As you decide on what it is you want to achieve, you can take conscious control of your mind and direct it in ways that best serves you. I will show you how to do this later in the book. You'll know how to make conscious choices that aligns to the life that you want to live. You'll no longer feel powerless to your circumstances, but know that you are a brilliant creator of your life. It does not have to be a difficult process, but one that you can do with ease, once you learn how to properly condition your mind and harness Universal Laws that govern our world to help you achieve your goals and dreams.

Who do you need to become?

When you start the journey to achieve your dreams, realize that the person you'll need to be to achieve it is not the person you are now. Your dreams will require you to shift and change. This will cause some resistance for you, because as you'll learn, your mind is designed to keep you safe and for you to stay within your comfort zone. Anything that requires change signals a threat and although the change is something you consciously want, the fear of change becomes frightening to you and as a result will cause you to want to stop.

Oftentimes, the test we go through in the quest for our goals will change us. It sure changed me. There was a point where things were so tough financially for me. I was working hard to achieve my dreams, but I felt like a complete failure and a fraud because I was teaching empowering principals, yet I was unable to feel financially secure. I realized that I was not living my teachings. I got it at an intellectual level and understood the concept, but I was not living it and not showing up fully. I was still hiding and not dreaming big and seeing myself as the person who's able to achieve their dreams. I had yet to see myself as that person.

I had to be different. It was only when I truly committed to work the practises that I'm sharing with you in this book, did my confidence rise. I was able to see all the many successes I had and trust in my power to transform my life. I took stock of the changes I was able to inspire in others and did not feel like a second-class version of anyone else. I saw myself as a first-class version of me and really owned it.

As a result, so-called coincidences took place, and opportunities started to present themselves and I felt great. I had an opportunity to co-produce and host my own television show that airs on my local community station, which was so well received by my viewers. Amazing new clients started coming into my business through an offering that utilized my knowledge and expertise and was unique to me. I really felt like I was getting paid to be me!

I stopped worrying about what others were thinking of me and really felt that those who followed me were meant to and those who didn't or un-followed me were okay in their choice to do so. It was not about me, but the fact that we weren't a match. There are billions of people on this planet and I know those who resonate with my work will be those who I am meant to serve.

You also have to learn to be bigger than your current circumstances. See yourself bigger and above your doubts and fears. That is who you need to become! Embrace your strength and power and harness it to its full potential. Trust me when I say you are powerful and capable of making anything happen that you set your mind to!

The Illusion of Time

Something I want to make sure I address is the illusion many of us have regarding time. The truth is, there is no such thing as time. Everything exists *only* in the present moment. Einstein proved that time is not an absolute, but relative. The key to conscious creation and being able to experience your desires is by accepting, embracing and honouring the present moment.

We try so hard to create a new reality for ourselves, yet often spend our lives reliving the past or being fearful about the future. We fail to recognize that the present moment is all we have, and where our power truly resides. It is in the present moment, are we able to manifest our goals.

When you're able to accept that the present moment is all you have, you're able to stop resisting and better able to accept what is. When you live your life from this place of peace and acceptance, your ability to manifest becomes more powerful. You then show up fully exactly where you're at, and give each moment all you've got!

The recognition that the only time that matters is now, allows you to stop waiting for the 'perfect' time to dare to go after your dreams. When you realize at a deep level that you don't have to wait to live your dreams, it opens up a whole new level of consciousness. A consciousness and awareness that whatever you want is always here, waiting for your recognition.

When you're able to find happiness and peace in the present moment, it guarantees that whatever you're pursuing will be fulfilling, because you're already content and happy. Anything else that comes as a result is only here to enrich your experience.

The biggest catalyst to success and fulfillment, both personally, and financially is your ability to consistently *be here now.*

When you start to learn how to create a new reality, sometimes you look to that end state and become dissatisfied with what is. The need to achieve your goals creates a contrast that leaves you frustrated and anxious. Like I just mentioned, where you are, is exactly where you need to be.

There's no need to chase anything outside of you. This work really is an inside job, one that begins with bringing more love, joy and attention to each moment. Don't get trapped in the illusion of time. We all have the same amount of time, yet how we use and experience it often differ. You can use your time to consciously create the life you want, by understanding that every moment is creating your future experiences. No more "I'll be happy when... or "I'll start tomorrow." Tomorrow never comes as the saying goes, so you must stop waiting for circumstances to change before receiving the abundance that already surrounds you.

Cultivating mindfulness will help you stay connected with the present moment. You can create more mindfulness in your life by living in the moment, and bringing awareness to the activities you typically do. Whatever you're doing, engage and give your full attention to it. Let go of regrets from the past and fears about the future. Just stay present with what is, trusting that what you desire will materialize at the right time.

Deep breathing is another simple and powerful exercise to help you stay in the moment. Focus on your breath as you inhale deeply and exhale slowly. Repeat several times and focus on connecting to your breath, relaxing and being at peace in the moment.

CHAPTER 3

Working with the Laws of the Universe

"There is an orderliness in the universe, there is an
unalterable law governing everything and every
being that exists or lives. It is no blind law; for no
blind law can govern the conduct of living beings."
~Mahatma Gandhi

I want to get into a topic that has the power to help you
create the change you want with more ease and support.
That is aligning with the universal laws that govern this
incredible universe that we live in.

Many people feel that they must struggle and work
really hard in order to manifest their goals. Now yes,
there is work involved and you may have to put in some
time, but something I've come to believe is that you do
not need to struggle.

Struggle is a word that people use so freely and
quickly. This was the case in my life. Growing up in a
single parent home with two other sisters and watching
my mother work very hard, I equated life with struggle,
because that is what I saw. I saw my mother struggle

daily to try and make ends meet. This belief became impressed in my subconscious and led to me feeling like I needed to struggle in my life. Even when I made great money, I always felt that I struggled financially.

Something that I learnt, that was a major game-changer for me was when I was introduced to Universal Laws. These are laws that govern our world and are always occurring regardless of our awareness to them or not. When we're able to understand these laws and harness them, then the achievement of our goals becomes so much easier and we can experience change much faster.

Like many people, the first time I came across the laws of the Universe was through the popular movie and book, *The Secret* and its introduction to the Law of Attraction. Now, when I first watched the movie and read the book, I did not realize that this Law of Attraction is one of many laws that govern our world. This is why many people felt that the Law of Attraction did not work for them. They fail to recognize and leverage other universal laws that are at play. Laws that when understood and applied, gives you the greatest impact to manifest your goals.

I'm going to use this part of the book to quickly touch upon some laws to take into consideration, as you become the deliberate creator of your life. There are many books written in great detail on the subject including Raymond Holliwell's *Working with the Law*. Another great resource is David Neagle's *The Millions Within*.

I want to highlight some key laws to understand and keep in mind that'll help you manifest easier and quickly. I will not go through the entire laws as I've said there are many great books out there that are more comprehensive on the subject. However, this summary will help you know how to make them work for you and narrow the gap to your goals.

Law of Vibration

The Law of Vibration is the primary law in which the Law of Attraction is built on. It's based on the fact that everything in our entire universe is made up of energy. When you see something as matter and solid, you're not seeing the true nature of it. When you look with a microscope and go to the deepest level of your being, you're made up of pure energy.

This energy is in constant motion and vibrates at different speeds and frequency. Nothing stands still and rests, including you, the book you hold in your hands and the chair you may be sitting on reading these words. Everything in the entire universe operates in this manner.

Understanding this law is instrumental to achieving and living your dreams because your thoughts and feelings also have a vibrational frequency. As I said, we vibrate at different rate of frequency. It starts in our thoughts, which influences our emotions. Your emotion controls the frequency at which you vibrate. Your frequency then determines what resonates or is 'attracted' to you (hence The Law of Attraction in action).

This law is powerful and it's important to understand how to make it work for you! When you have a goal, vision or dream for yourself, and you begin to think about it and feel how it would be like to have it, that vibration aligns with like vibrations and draws them into your life. Remember the cycle of reality when based on your focus, stories, realities etc., you began to see evidence of the same?

If you want to know what you're vibrating, then check in with your feeling and emotions. The way you feel is a clear indication of what is coming into your awareness and being attracted to you, and thus comes the Law of Attraction.

Law of Attraction

The Law of Attraction is probably the most common law that people know thanks to the aforementioned film and book *The Secret*. However, as I've written, this Law of Attraction is oftentimes misunderstood.

The Law of Attraction simply states that 'like attracts like'. Whatever you think and focus on is what you'll attract into your life. Now, the truth behind this law is that it is more about *awareness*. Whatever you give your attention to will be expanded into your awareness. You'll become more aware of it.

Your thoughts influence your feelings and emotions and it is through your emotions that you vibrate. The frequency at which you vibrate equals your point of attraction.

Your vibration lets you know what you're focused on. When you're in a low level frequency like guilt, anger and fear, your level of awareness is focused on the problem. The issue most people have when trying to manifest their dreams and reach their goals is that instead of holding onto the vision and thoughts of what they want, and tuning into the feeling of it, they change frequencies. They align with doubt, fear and scarcity. They switch their frequencies so often that by the time their manifestation starts to head toward them, they're no longer in the frequency to receive it. As a result, they don't see it, nor allow themselves to receive it.

In order to utilize this law and allow it to work in your favour, you need to continue to hold the vision and maintain the frequency long enough to see the opportunity that will present itself to you for its attainment. This is why you hear so much about practicing gratitude. If you have a daily gratitude practice, it helps you maintain alignment for like vibrations to come into your awareness.

How many times have you tried to reach a goal and make something happen, however, because it feels like it's taking too long, you stop? You then become filled with doubt, fear and lack. This feeling of doubt, fear and lack now becomes what you're aligned too and consequently you no longer are on the path to achieving what it is you say you want.

When you utilize The Law of Attraction, whatever you predominantly focus and think about will be brought into your awareness. The first step is to start consciously thinking and focusing on what it is you want.

The Struggle with the Law of Attraction

Like I mentioned at the beginning of this book, I really started to research and committed to learning about how we create our reality when I first came across *The Secret* on *The Oprah Show*.

I remember thinking it was everything I've always believed and hoped for, all packaged in this little gift called The Secret and The Law of Attraction. I got to work putting into practise what was taught in order to manifest my greatest dreams. At that time, I was working on plans to open up my wellness center with my sister and the company I was working for just announced the biggest lay-off it has ever seen. Now for most people, this would have been the worst news, but for me it was the greatest. You see I had already planned to leave to start my business, so I saw this as a sign that I could use the creation process to manifest being laid off. At the time, I worked for the company for about 13 years, so the package would have been enough to help fund the start up of my business. I believed I had this!

Well, let's just say that little plan of mine did not work out and left me hurt and devastated. I know, the irony of this, when others were devastated to lose jobs they relied so heavily on. For me, I knew working in the corporate world was not for me, regardless of the great wage they paid me. I had other plans and wanted the freedom to work for myself and make a greater impact on the world through my work and business.

I also thought that the fact that *The Secret* came into my life when it did, was so I could manifest a package. As I look back now, I see many mistakes I made in trying to manifest it, including being so attached to the outcome. This is one that many people make when they go on the quest to manifesting their dreams using The Law of Attraction.

When we don't see the manifestation of what we want, we begin to think that The Law of Attraction does not work and that we're failing in some way to use it. The truth is though that no one fails at the Law of Attraction, just like you cannot *fail* at the law of gravity. If you walk off a building, you cannot 'fail' to fall down and hurt yourself or worse.

Most people forget that the Law of Attraction is based on the Law of Vibration. Your habitual thoughts influence your emotions, which in turn controls the frequency you vibrate, as I explained earlier. So it's not your thoughts that draw things into your life, but actually your feelings and emotions. I'll get into this in more detail, but understand that the role your thoughts play in the manifestation process is that it is a great influencer of your feelings, and your feelings are the magnet that draws things into your life.

As I look back now on trying to manifest a package, I was full of anxiety over it. I wanted it, but there was this nervousness. Also, I was focused that it had to be 'that way!' Even though I didn't manifest a package and ended up quitting, and yes we faced difficult times during the launch of our wellness centre, we got through it! There were different opportunities that presented itself to help us through the start up phase.

So if you're saying hundreds of affirmations a day, yet focused and thinking about what's wrong in your life and feeling fearful that your desire and goals will not manifest, then truly you won't see the manifestation of what you want.

Another big reason why you may feel that The Law of Attraction isn't working, is that you're trying to manifest from a place of lack. If you feel you don't have it, then you'll continue to not have it. Again, no amount of affirmations will help. You need to come from a place of abundance knowing that you already have everything you need to make it happen. If you have a desire for something, then you MUST have the resources and abilities to manifest it. If you did not, then you would not have had the desire in the first place. This is what the Law of Polarity states, which I'll delve into shortly.

Feeling like something is missing continues to perpetrate more conditions of things being missing from your life. Consequently, the very thing you want to manifest will continue to elude you.

You may also feel that The Law of Attraction is not working for you because your subconscious beliefs and program conflict with what you want. I see this a lot when it comes to money, myself included! If you're not seeing the physical manifestation of your desires, then subconsciously, you're resisting it.

How many times have you heard 'money is the root of all evil', or 'making money is hard', and 'people like you can't get rich', to even one that came up for me around how 'being rich is unsafe'? All of these programs are outside of your conscious awareness, but undermine your efforts to have more money or anything else that you desire. So you try to use the Law of Attraction to manifest, however your subconscious mind is in opposition, and your core beliefs go against what you want. As a result, you don't get the physical manifestation of it.

You need to ensure that your *conscious* desires (thoughts) are in alignment with your subconscious beliefs and the actions that you take. Once you have alignment, then you'll begin to manifest what you want quickly and with ease.

I will be sharing some tools and techniques you can use to re-program your mind to align with what you want later in this book. For now, know that if you've tried to manifest something and felt you 'failed' at it, it's because your subconscious mind was not in alignment with what it is you said you wanted to have.

Another area where people feel that The Law of Attraction, or any manifestation strategies for that matter is not working for them is in the time it takes for them to see their manifestation. The biggest misconception is that people feel that nothing is happening, when *indeed* it is working. Here's the thing, the manifestation process starts in the invisible realm. When you activate the process (by holding onto the vision and taking on the feeling of what you want) you ignite the creation process. You will not see it externally, but things begin to happen that are outside of your current awareness.

Instead of focusing on your desires and having faith and trusting the process, you begin to get frustrated and feel disappointed. Frustration and disappointment are low-level frequencies and so you must be in the same vibrational frequency as your desires in order to receive it. Your goals and dreams were indeed coming to you, but because you're no longer in the same vibrational frequency (remember the Law of Vibration), you are unable to receive what you wanted to manifest. Consequently, you concluded that The Law Of Attraction was not working for you, when in reality it was!

Another great misuse of this law is in focusing on the *how* instead of the *what*. Your job in the creation process is to focus on *what* you want to manifest. Have faith and believe that you will receive what you want.

Don't focus on how this will come about. The 'how' is up to God/Universe. When you focus on the how, you bring your limited consciousness into the equation. I love what Mike Dooley says in The Secret when he states, 'The "hows" are the domain of the Universe. It always knows the shortest, quickest, fastest, most harmonious way between you and your dream."

The techniques you've been taught are indeed correct, however, you may have let outside circumstances or your past conditioning keep you out of alignment from *receiving* your goals. But, as you go through the pages of this book and put to practice what's laid out for you, you'll indeed bridge the gap from where you are to where you want to be.

In order to achieve, manifest or obtain your goal, you need to look into the Law of Cause and Effect.

Law of Cause and Effect

This is one of my favourite laws because it's the basis of how we achieve and create. The Law of Cause and Effect states that for every effect there is a cause and for every cause there's an effect. So if you want more money, a loving relationship, and a fulfilling career, well that's an effect. However, to obtain it, there is a cause that's needed to make it happen.

You've probably heard, 'you reap what you sow'. This is based on the notion that for every action there is an equal and opposite reaction. Your thoughts, words and actions cause the results of what you see and experience in your reality. It is through this law that you're able to manifest what you set your mind to.

Harness this law by looking at the causes of what it is you want to achieve, and taking action to its attainment. Start focusing on the causes you want, and thus having a direct influence on the outcome. Whatever you send into the Universe comes back to you; start choosing to do the things that will get you the success you desire. When you start to take action, take inventory of the consequences of your actions and decisions. Will they take you closer to your dream? Will it bring you a sense of joy and fulfillment?

Remember all these laws work in tandem. So if you become aware and start taking the right 'actions' to bring you to your goals, but you're still focused on what's wrong, missing or lacking, and feeling badly for it, you won't get what it is you truly desire. The Law of Vibration brings you things that match your feelings.

What happens to many people is that they begin to take action towards their dreams, but as part of the journey they are met with some form of resistance. The resistance is created by your subconscious mind to keep you in your comfort zone. What you need to do is stay focused and commit to the work you need to do and keep going. Don't focus on your past programs and issues that developed to keep you stuck. Stay focused on your vision and take action towards your goals. These are the exact causes that'll bring you to your dreams. If you have a desire, then the ability to manifest it is already present, which is what the Law of Polarity teaches.

From Aspiration to Fulfillment

Law of Polarity

The law of polarity is something I came across from one of my teachers, David Neagle. He speaks about this law quite a bit and I have to admit it took me time to grasp the true meaning of it and how I was able to use it to achieve my goals.

Law of Polarity states that 'everything that exists has an equal and exact opposite'. You cannot perceive something to be good without the perception of bad, nor would you know how to experience success without the presence of failure. How would you know what happiness is, if you did not know the feeling of sadness?

This means that if you're in a situation right now that you're dissatisfied with, and want to change, the seed and ability to change is already present. The opposite (what you want), already exists. 'For anything to exist, there has to be an equal and exact opposite.'

To illustrate this further, I want to share a quote I recently came across by Chuck Danes. He says, "Within the darkest of life's perceived trials and hardships lies the means as well as the ability to find and experience the light." Napoleon Hill in his classic book Think & Grow Rich, also explains this law beautifully when he said, 'Every adversity, every failure, and every heartache carries with it the seed of an equivalent or greater benefit.'

So let's take an example that many people are familiar with, and that is lack of financial stability. If you find yourself constantly struggling with money and find that you're unable to keep up with your expenses, then it means that because this 'lack' is in your consciousness;

the opposite of it, the part where you're financially secure *also* exists. You cannot have one without the other.

To apply this law in order to close the gap to your dreams is to understand that whatever desire you have in your heart, the ability to manifest it already exists. If you feel the absence of it and desire it, that means the presence of it and a version where you have it, is also true and available.

I know this may seem hard to perceive because you've been used to seeing what is and the lack of what you desire. However, the presence of your desire is already here, because if it were not, you would not have felt the desire in the first place. The ability to bring it about already exists, just outside of your present awareness.

What you need to do in order to bring it into your awareness is to harness the Law of Attraction by focusing on what you desire until it comes into your awareness. Remember these laws do not operate independent of one another. They are interdependent and work harmoniously with each other.

Another thing I love about this law is that anytime I'm feeling stuck and feel that I do not know the next step, it reminds me that the 'knowing' is available to me. So many times, people say they don't know what they want. Well, you can start by taking note of what you *don't* want, and what you want will naturally reveal itself to you.

Another application of this law is that in the midst of the storm, there is something positive to be found in it. Most times, it's when the storm has passed are we able to learn the lesson because we're less emotionally involved with it. However, when we look back the lessons and benefits existed then.

This was something I also learnt from my trainer and master coach, Mark Fournier. Through his program Life Mastery, which I later facilitated, there was a lesson called 'Everything Always Works Out', which my participants lovingly called EAWO. There was an exercise I had participants do that took them back to events and situations that they felt were painful and they were to write out how it worked out.

What this exercise did was to illustrate that no matter what the events were, there was something positive that came out of it. If you really look and focus on solutions instead of the problems, you'll indeed find it!

To illustrate this further, I want to share a personal story about a launch I once had. This was a program that was so dear to my heart and I put a lot of work into. I also invested money in technology that would deliver a great learning experience for participants.

Now in theory, I did everything right. I read a book based on launching and thought I had the process down pat. I watched countless webinars, took courses and followed the process as described. I was so excited about the launch and the money that would come as a result. Now, keep in mind that I just left a company where my salary with bonuses went into the six-figure mark. I also had some debts and payments I needed to make. But I was sure that this launch was it, and with the process I was following, I would pay it all back, plus money to sustain me. And guess what. Want to know how many sales I made during the launch? Ready for it? 0!!! Absolutely nothing!

To say I was shocked and disappointed was an understatement. I later sold one, but the launch and program felt like a complete failure! People were so excited and loved the concept, plus I had great results from my beta launch. However, the actual launch was a complete bust! Or so it seemed.

As I look back on the experience, I can tell you with absolute confidence that I gained so much from it. There was an intern who was supporting me with this launch. This girl became a huge support for me and paramount to my business. She is extremely talented and someone who is core to my business.

Furthermore, I was able to use a lot of the content from my program in this book you now hold in your hands. I'm now able to see the seeds of opportunities from that failed launched.

The biggest seed from that launch that caused the biggest shift for me was that it forced me to become a student of my work. I committed to regular practice of the lessons I'm now sharing with you. I was so focused on what I was supposed to 'do' to launch the program versus who I was *being*. I started connecting back to Source and trusting God for my income and needs. I placed so much emphasis on the results of my launch that I lost sight of what was important. I didn't listen to my intuition and what felt good, and just did what the 'experts' told me I should be doing. As a result, it didn't work out. However, the law of polarity was still in place, because the seed and opportunity to get what I truly wanted was present, within it. I got an amazing resource in my business and it also led me to work in a way that felt more aligned and true to me.

CHAPTER 4

The Marvellous Working of your Mind

"Thoughts become things. If you see it in your
mind, you will hold it in your hand."
~Bob Proctor

I want to take this time and dedicate this chapter to briefly explain about how marvellous our minds really are and their role in helping us achieve our goals. I've referred to both the conscious and subconscious mind throughout this book so far, and I want to make sure you understand exactly how it works and how you can use it to achieve your goals.

Like I've mentioned, your subconscious mind is the biggest factor that influences the results you currently have. This is how powerful your mind is. When you're able to harness the power of your mind, plus living harmoniously with the laws of the Universe, the results are remarkable and miraculous!

I have to admit when I first learnt about the power of my subconscious mind to manifest my greatest desires it was something that I understood, again, at an intellectual level. Only until I truly understood this information at my core and integrated it into my life was I able to harness the power to see real transformation.

In order to use this powerful part of you to create results, let's first examine how it's shaped the reality you now experience. With this new knowledge, you can then use your mind to create what you truly want.

In this section, I'm going to explain the different levels of the mind, and how it's worked to give you the results you currently have. I'll also show you how to recondition your mind to get what you want.

The Nature of your Mind

Everything you now see and experience is what your mind has been programmed to believe to be true. If you experience lack of money, failing relationship, and constant struggle, then this is what your mind believes to be true (money is hard to get, relationships don't last, and life is hard).

Over the years and especially through childhood, your mind has been exposed to many impressions. These impressions are stored within your subconscious mind and became the reality you now experience.

Your mind is spiritual in nature. It's not physical like the brain, but unseen just like your thoughts. It's a dualistic being made up of the conscious mind and subconscious mind. There is also a third level called the superconscious mind, which I will explain more about in a bit, but for now I'll focus on the conscious and subconscious mind.

Your conscious mind is often referred to as the 'reasoning' mind. This is because it is through your conscious mind that you're able to make decisions. You choose your home, what to eat, etc. through your conscious reasoning. Although this conscious part of your mind 'reasons', it has the least effect on your current conditions. If I ask you a complex mathematical equation like, 100 divided by 20, you'd have to think about it a little. It requires you thinking and thus, your conscious mind is also known as the 'thinking' mind.

Your subconscious mind however, drives what shows up in your life. This is where your memories and habits are stored. It's greatly influenced by the conscious mind as it 'takes orders' through it. It accepts what is impressed upon it. This impression happens over time and with constant repetition. Going back to the math example, if I asked you for the sum of 1+1, you'd automatically say 2. This is because you've heard 1+1 so often that your subconscious mind automatically comes up with 2. You automatically came up with that answer without much thought to it.

Another great example often used to explain the two is when you first learnt how to drive. At first, you really had to think about it and concentrate and were so conscious and alert to the lessons being taught to you. However, years after learning to drive, your subconscious takes over. You don't have to consciously think about it. You just pop the keys in the ignition and take off!

Your subconscious mind accounts for 80-95% of the results you see in your life. Take a look at the results you have in all areas of your life. They are all based on your beliefs. The beliefs your subconscious mind holds onto were placed there based on your habitual thoughts, words, feelings and action. Again, most of the programs were developed before the age of seven.

I love the way Bob Proctor explains the duality of our minds. Before the age of seven, our mind was made up of only the lower half, the subconscious mind. All ideas went directly into this subconscious mind like the open vessel I spoke of earlier. After the age of seven, our beliefs are then formed based on what was presented to us. We then develop our conscious mind. When new ideas are later presented to us, the conscious mind would 'reason' with it. If it was not consistent with what we believe to be true about ourselves (within our subconscious mind), we simply reject it.

This is why some people have a hard time making the change they want in their lives. They consciously want to change and when they're presented with new ideas like, 'you can change your life' and 'you have the power to be and do whatever you like', those ideas are quickly rejected. These new ideas are inconsistent with your beliefs and past programming and, as a result, get discarded.

Like I mentioned prior with the mishaps of The Law of Attraction, many people try a lot of techniques and get frustrated at the results. This is why so many people who attempted to use the creation process (ask, believe, receive) presented in the movie The Secret were unsuccessful. They didn't succeed to make their desires a reality because they missed the second step, which is to *believe*. Belief is where the subconscious mind comes into play.

If you tried to utilize The Law of Attraction without

success, it's because you may have thought you believed in the process and your ability to manifest your goals, however, subconsciously, you did not. Your subconscious rejected it, because you had unconscious beliefs that opposed what it was you were trying to manifest.

Even though you were repeating your affirmations, creating the vision boards and doing what was asked, your current programming was not a match. The results you get in your life is based on what your subconscious mind believes to be true, so affirmations will not make an immediate impact if your mind is filled with opposing beliefs.

You will experience the results of the beliefs held within your subconscious mind. What it believes to be true is experienced in your physical world (proof). The sad part is, that oftentimes, these beliefs are not only limiting, but they are outside of your awareness. If you want to know what your beliefs are, then look at the results you have in your life.

Your subconscious mind acts like a soil that accepts the seeds you plant in it; the seeds being your habitual thoughts. It accepts the seeds, whether that seed is good or bad (positive or negative thoughts). It takes whatever is impressed upon it, and acts to bring it about.

The paradox of this is that your programming (which is also another name for habits) is what's giving you the results you currently have. However, it's difficult to change those habits, but once they're changed, it automatically gives you the results you want.

Your mind is also greatly influenced by what is repeatedly impressed upon it. Again, this is why affirmations work for some and not for others. If you're subconscious program does not oppose what you wish to manifest and create, then it'll sink in and respond to it. However, most people have deep and strong blocks against what they want, and that is why affirmations don't work in the short term.

The Superconscious Mind

I mentioned briefly about the concept/idea of the superconscious mind. This is a term that may not be familiar to you, as people often speak (myself included) about the duality of the mind and focus on the conscious and subconscious mind. Now, there is a third component to the mind that I want to take a little time to share with you.

Many have often referred to this part of the mind as your Higher Self, Spirit, Soul, etc. Again, I don't want to get caught up on labels, but on the power it has to help you in the fulfillment of your desires.

One of my all-time favourite personal development teachers, the late great metaphysician Florence Scovel Shinn, calls this part of the mind 'the Christ within'.

In her book, *The Secret Door to Success*, she writes about the Superconscious mind: "The superconscious is the realm of inspiration, revelation, illumination and intuition... The superconscious is the realm of perfect ideas. The great genius captures his thoughts from the superconscious."

What I believe about this part of the mind is that it connects our subconscious mind to our Creator. It is the source that powers our subconscious mind to carry out the orders and beliefs within it. It is God/Source within.

This part of the mind is associated with intuition and creativity, and connects us to all living beings in our world. It's the part of us that knows no limits and you're able to access through deep meditation or with the consistent practice of alignment.

For me, this superconscious presence comes and goes in my life. I can't say it is something I consistently feel connected to, because I've yet to reach the enlightened state that allows me to feel its presence on a consistent basis. However, the presence is always there, waiting for me to connect to it and assist me in moving past my limiting beliefs.

Aligning your Beliefs

It's important to understand that even though many people have been programmed with limiting beliefs, it can be changed and altered. You can indeed overcome negative patterns that are running your life.

Awareness is a great starting point. It allows you to understand the causes of your current circumstances. This new understanding gives you the ability to create the change you want.

The same way that your mind acts out the programs that is implanted within it, once you're able to replace them with new ones, your life will begin to change. It will change quickly and easily once you implant new thought patterns into your subconscious mind that leads you to your goals.

The subconscious mind responds greatly to repetition and emotion. These are the two biggest factors of influence.

When you focus on what you want and stay consistent with your focus, you'll start to change the nature of your thinking, and the way your brain behaves.

I'm not a neuro-scientist, nor do I want this book to be technical in nature, but I do want to quickly touch upon the brain and mind connection. The brain and mind relationship is a complex topic with some differing views depending on where you look. Although, the terms 'brain' and 'mind' are often interchanged, and are intimately connected, experts agree that there is indeed a difference. Your mind as I mentioned before, stores your thoughts, beliefs, memories, attitude and habits, and is non-physical. It permeates every cell of your being, and not just your brain cells.

Your brain on the other hand is a physical part of your body that controls and coordinates 'mental and physical actions'. New scientific discoveries are constantly being made about this complex area of our body, but it is through the brain that information is perceived and directed. Professor at UCLA medical school, Dan Siegel, explains it this way; "The mind can use the brain to perceive itself, and the mind can be used to change the brain." So, you can focus your mind to change the way your brain behaves to be in alignment to your goals.

When you continue to focus on what you want, and who you want to be, you start to develop new thought patterns, habits and behaviors, which leads to the change you want. When you change the way you think, you change the physical structure of your brain, because parts of your brain are flexible, adaptable and open to change.

Something I learnt from Marissa Peers, a leading UK Therapist, is that, your brain does what it thinks you want it to do, so it's up to you to tell it what you truly desire. Again, you tell it through your thoughts, words and emotions.

Our brain is trained to reject anything that is unfamiliar, as it sees it as a threat. This is going back to the hunter and gathering days when our brain signals for us to flee when approached by a wild and dangerous animal. However, this same behaviour is used today. Instead of fleeing from an unknown animal, we flee from doing new things that will lead us to our goals, because it's new and unfamiliar to us. Chances are your aspiration is something you've never experienced before. It is unknown to you. As a result, your brain will reject it, because success, being something *new*, is threatening to it.

This can be as big as leaving a job that no longer serves you in order to start a business based on your passion. This was the case for me. It was absolutely scary leaving a job that I built a lucrative career in, and leaving it for a second time to work from home. There were so many reasons to stay including a great salary, a growing family, and no guarantee that my program would succeed, which by the way, my first launch was a complete failure! Yet I still survived it.

Your fear can also be in the form of stepping out, meeting someone that can lead to a fulfilling relationship that you dream of. However, you resist either agreeing to be set up, going to places where you'll meet people, or possibly creating your profile on a reputable dating site. Your mind tells you that it is not safe to do so.

49

Inner and Outer Dialogue

I want to now share some tools and techniques that you can use to impress new beliefs from your conscious mind to your subconscious mind in order to get what you really want.

One of the best ways to change your subconscious program is through your thoughts and words. This is the same way you built your beliefs and as such the way you can implant new ones.

At the start of this book, you identified your habitual thoughts and beliefs. You identified those that served and those that did not serve you. In order to change and impress new beliefs, you need to change what you've been feeding your mind.

Your thoughts and words need to align to what you wish to have happen in your life. Remember thoughts are real. They carry an emotional charge that affects what you bring into your life.

According to Physician Larry Dossey, a leader in mind-body medicine, thoughts "cause biological and physiological effects. Your body responds to mental input as if it were physically real." I like to interpret the impact of your thoughts as the following:

Your thoughts affect your feelings. Your feelings affect your actions (remember we behave in accordance to how we feel). Your actions influence your life experience.

Based on the above it's important to be cautious of what you focus on, think and talk about. Notice the dialogue going on inside your mind, and ones you are speaking out loud either to yourself and others about your life and what you're able to achieve. Are you constantly discussing and complaining about all the things that are wrong in the world? Do you watch the news first thing in the morning and before you go to bed and fill your consciousness with all the negative reporting that fills up the news? Yes, you need to be informed, but many people inundate themselves with so much negative programs and energy from the media. All of this impacts your mind and what you think about.

Remember your thoughts play a big role in the way you feel. Your feelings are a powerful way to attract things into your life. It's not necessarily your thoughts of abundance that brings it into your life, but rather your *feelings* of abundance. Your feelings are an energetic magnet that draws like things to you through the Law of Attraction. Your emotional energetic state will be mirrored in your future, as your future is created by who you're being right now.

The Universe will match the feelings and emotions you're emitting. You're not attracting, what you want, rather what you're being. Your emotions are critical to the manifestation and achievement of your goals. So, if you're feeling abundant and prosperous, then you will draw more of that into your life. However, you can't feel abundant and prosperous without first *thinking* about and focusing on abundance and prosperity!

The Power of I AM!

Another powerful technique I also use is being cautious of the way I speak when using the words "I am". I AM is the Biblical name for God, and regardless of your spiritual or religious background or faith, it's important to understand the impact it has on your ability to attract what you want into your life.

Typically, we use the word *I am* in such a way that does not serve us. Think about what typically follows your "I am"..... Most of the time, it's negative. We often say *I am* tired, *I am* sick, *I am* too young, *I am* too old, *I am* poor, and the list goes on! I love what I heard Pastor Joel Osteen say when he was on Super Soul Sunday. He said, "Whatever follows your I am will come looking for you." It will bring more of the same things into your life. Become conscious and choose words that best serve you! You can start off with something that you can buy into so your ego does not resist you and then build on it from there. If you are $50,000 in debt instead of saying I am a millionaire you can say, "I am open to the abundance that's available to me. I am worthy of new and exciting opportunities to make more money". Or "I welcome the opportunity for my debt to be eliminated."

Think of some affirmations that resonate with you based on what you want to happen in your life.

Affirming your new Reality

In order to change your circumstance, you have to see every thought you think as seeds you're sowing into the fertile soil of your mind. Your mind controls your circumstances and what you implant will be experienced.

Affirmations are powerful to use to change your current conditions and implant seeds of what you wish to manifest. You can reinforce your desired outcome with positive words, thoughts, and affirmations. They're great tools to use to convince your subconscious mind that what you want to achieve is already a done deal!

Take whatever it is you want and repeat it constantly to yourself. Take the end goal and fulfillment of your goals and repeat them to yourself. Many people will argue that affirmations don't work for them. The truth is that they are right, in one sense. Affirmations did not work for them because they were not persistent in their use of affirmation. They did not stick with it long enough for it to sink into their consciousness. They did not do it enough to re-wire the way their brain thinks.

Another reason why affirmations may have not worked for them is they may have started, and something happened that impacted their goal and they got frustrated and upset, thus contradicting and erasing the work that was being done through the affirmations. Remember your emotions are very powerful and are bringing like vibrations into your life and awareness.

What you need to do is consistently persist in using your affirmations. You may also experience some resistance, which you can clear with tools that I'll be sharing later in the book.

It's okay if you're unable to emotionalize your affirmations at first, especially if they're yet to feel believable to you. Keep going and in time it will begin to sink in. Your mind will begin to buy into it over time. You'll then begin to experience seemingly coincidental events that bring you opportunities to attain your goals. Do not dismiss these events and circumstances, as they are part of your answered prayers.

Making your affirmations work for you

You can use affirmations already created by others, as there many great ones found online. You can also write ones yourself that are more personal to what it is you want to achieve.

To maximize the power of affirmations, I want to give you some guidelines when creating them. When you start to create affirmations in order to bring in what you desire, ensure you:

- State it in the present tense. If you say, "I will reach my desired income", the word *will* keeps it in the future and not registering to your mind that it's happening right now. What you can say is something like, "I am now making more than enough to satisfy my needs."
- Use positive wording. Instead of affirming, "I am not in debt," say, "I am financially abundant" or "I am open to the flow of money." Don't affirm what you don't want. Keep the phrase within a positive word-frame so that your subconscious doesn't absorb any negative words.
- Evoke feelings of possibility within yourself and imagine your dream actually coming true. The feeling of expectation and possibility is the magnet that draws it to you. Find ways to make this feeling more powerful. Feel more emotionally connected to your affirmation, because that is going to be the catalyst that turns your dreams into reality.

I cannot stress enough the importance of maintaining your affirmations. It is said that repetition is the mother of all learning and this is absolutely true. When you consistently repeat your affirmations either out loud or in your head, you begin to impress the new thoughts into your subconscious mind. You begin to rewire your brain and establish new sets of beliefs; ones that are aligned to what you want. With enough repetition and emotion, you'll begin to see change. It begins slowly, but once your dominant thoughts and beliefs are consistent with what you consciously want, that is where the magic happens. You will begin to see the physical manifestation of what you want.

CHAPTER 5

The Power of your Imagination

"Cherish your visions and your dreams
as they are the children of your soul, the
blueprints of your ultimate achievements."
~Napoleon Hill

In this chapter, I'll share with you the techniques and tools to start narrowing the gap to your dreams. The use of our imagination is one of the quickest and best ways to do this. No matter what you want to achieve, if you can picture it in your mind and it feels natural to you, then you have the ability and capability to make it real.

You must be clear about what you wish to manifest into your life. What does the end goal look like? If you wish to live an extraordinary miraculous life, then you need to be able to SEE it in your mind before it manifests in physical form. I like to compare it to a map. If you're looking to go on a trip and have a map that is fuzzy and not clear, what are the chances that you will reach your destination? Very unlikely, right?

This is the same for fulfilling your greatest desires.

You need to see a clear picture of what that life looks like. What are you doing? Who are you with? What is your day filled with? Clearly see it and believe it in order to have it in physical form.

Imagination and visualization are powerful tools to help you attain your goals. Athletes have used it for years to achieve success. Visualizing your dream life invokes powerful emotions that activate the Law of Attraction to bring the means to achieve it into your awareness.

Some people believe they have a hard time using their imagination and visualizing when the fact is, they do it all the time! Just in a way that does not serve them. Let me ask, how many times have you worried about something that has yet to happen. Whether your finances, health, relationship, or career, you name it. You worry about something happening in the future. Well, this is indeed using your imagination to visualize what you *don't* want to happen!

I've seen this with people when they begin to worry about their jobs when a lay-off is announced. Those people I've seen in constant worry ended up being part of the group that got laid off.

I know many times when I'm anxious about an important meeting and I worry about traffic and being late, I'd get caught in traffic and seem to catch every red light possible. Or as I try and grab a quick coffee, I'd inevitable choose the longer drive-thru line and be more delayed. This was using my imagination to manifest what I didn't want.

A Parallel Universe

One of the things I've come to believe is in the concept of a parallel universe. This means that there are different outcomes at any given time to an event and the ones we experience are ones that we give the most attention and focus to. I know this will be a hard concept for you to believe, but bear with me for a moment.

Whatever it is you want to accomplish is already a done deal. The possibility of it exists. It's happening right now and for you to experience it requires you to focus, think about it consistently and be a vibrational match to it. When you do this, your brain picks up on it and it feels like you're having it now, even though all you're doing is imagining. You actually begin to feel good in your body, as if something great is happening, but you don't know what. You have yet to see it. This feeling is a result of your brain registering this change and as a result you feel as though it's happening and this very feeling is the catalyst that makes it manifest much faster!

This thought of my desires already being fulfilled and existing in another reality or dimension helped my visualization practice and led me to want to do it more often. I used to think I had a hard time visualizing and seeing myself having and doing what I want. When I started to daydream I almost cut myself off as if to not 'jinx' it. When I realized that my goal and dream is happening, just from me thinking about it, it gave me the confidence to allow myself to 'go there'. To see and feel myself living the way I wanted.

When I deepened my belief in the existence of a parallel universe and that it is happening, I wanted to see more of that version of me and feel what that Uchechi was like! It was a version of me that was happy, wealthy, fit and could buy anything I wanted and give to others as generous and lavishly as I wanted. It felt so good to know that the more I thought about it the more I was drawing it into my life. It gave me the freedom to keep dreaming.

There are different alternatives and versions of your life that you can experience. However, the one you now find yourself in is based on the thoughts and emotions you've offered up. I love how Abraham-Hicks describes it in a video I came across. She said, "With every thought that you utter or offer, you set a reality in motion, and there are other beings, physically and non-physically focused, who are the characters that play out these scenarios....Every thought that you think, every thought that you contemplate, every word that you articulate, every gathering that you involve yourself in, every time you watch a television program, any time you participate with thought, within anything, you're setting the course of future realities somewhere."

This shows the power of your thoughts, words and focus on creating the reality that you consciously want to experience. What you pay attention and give focus to, will manifest and be experienced.

Dream Big

In the past, I realized that during the times when I struggled the most, was the times that I played it safe. I've had in my vision board and around my office that I wanted to make $25,000 a month. Now because circumstances were nowhere near that, my mind went to just being able to make enough to 'make ends meet'. The grand vision was replaced with how I can make the minimum and start from there.

Now there is nothing wrong with gradually moving up and to be honest, I think it is the best approach and I'll touch upon that later, however, what I was doing was dismissing the notion of living a $25,000 a month lifestyle. My consciousness and thinking was filled with just 'making enough'. That was my goal and all I wanted to do.

What happens is that the reality of 'making enough' in addition to the possibility of me making $25,000/month exists at the same time. With my focus and attention to just making 'enough' I was choosing *that* reality versus the one I really wanted which was to make $25,000/month.

The thing is that just making enough did nor stir me and wasn't exciting enough for me to be emotionally connected to it. The thought of making just enough, did not move me into action and did not feel pleasurable. In fact, all my brain registered was 'just enough' and I was filled with thoughts of what happened if I didn't have enough; then lack and scarcity thinking would set in. This actually delayed me from even manifesting 'just enough', let alone the abundant feeling that came with making $25,000/month. As a result, I felt stuck and frustrated.

What I'm asking you to do is hold the grand vision of the life you want. The ultimate goal. See it and become emotionally involved with it. This allows you to begin to draw circumstances and opportunities to help you achieve it. The great thing is that when you begin to see yourself living that life, it feels SO GOOD. You start to embody the emotions even though it has yet to manifest. Those emotions feel so strong and may oftentimes bring you to tears, as it did for me. Those strong emotions are your signal and message that your desire is crystalizing and turning into form.

If you continue to act in this matter regardless of curve balls that may be thrown at you, and the contrast of where you currently stand to where you want to be, you'll begin to narrow the gap.

The Why behind the What

When you start declaring what it is you want to have and be, it's important to always know the *why* behind your what. Your why is the powerful reasons you want to achieve your goals.

Knowing your why is so vital in everything you do. It's the fuel that helps keep you focused in the face of adversity, which always comes up when you take on anything that takes you outside your comfort zone. In order to fulfill your aspirations, you'll be called to do things that feel uncomfortable to you. When you look at the real reasons you want something, it helps you make sure that you're aspiring to the right things. Many times we set goals that may not be aligned to our true values. When you dig deep and uncover the layers of what you want, it helps you move towards something that resonates and feels natural to you. When you do this, you'll more likely feel supported and in the flow because you're moving towards your soul's calling.

This is why I love the work of Danielle LaPorte and her book, *Desire Map*, that talks about 'core desire feelings' (CDF), and thought it was genius and the ticket that actually guarantees that you strive for the right goals and ones that you'll actually enjoy pursuing.

The Desire Map's concept is that, because we set a goal in order to *feel* a certain way, we need to start from there (the feeling place). "You're not chasing the goal itself; you're actually chasing the *feeling* that you hope achieving that goal will give you." She calls these feelings, your *core desire feeling*.

When you take this approach, you'll then set goals based on how you want to feel. Take some goals you've previously set for yourself in the past. If I asked you, "why did you want it", it really boils down to a feeling.

Let's take a goal many people set, which is to lose weight. Let's say you want to lose 20lbs. Is it really about 20lbs itself or more how losing 20lbs would make you feel? Chances are, you want to lose 20lbs to feel fit, strong, healthy, confident and sexy. That's the goal you're really going after, not just the number on the scale. So, before you set your goals and aspirations, determine how those goals will make you feel first. Let that be your focus!

Setting your goals this way also helps you avoid subscribing to society's definition of what success and achievement should be. You don't want to find yourself reaching for something that is not important to you, nor makes you feel great. What does success and fulfilling your dreams feel like for you? Align your goals to those feelings.

If you take the example of losing 20lbs, and focused on the core desire feelings of being strong, fit, confident and sexy, you can set goals to strength train and work out 3-5x/week, because that's what it will take to *feel* that way versus just having a goal to lose 20lbs. Even buying a cute little black dress that hugs all the right places will give you the same feeling. And by the Law of Attraction, you'll begin to attract more things and opportunities to help you continue feeling the same way.

Another great thing about this is that it allows you to evaluate opportunities that come up for you. It helps you stay on track and remain focused on what you want to achieve.

You may have heard of the "shiny object" syndrome, which is basically being drawn to the next best thing, thus distracting you from your goals and commitments. However, if you have something to compare the opportunities against, it makes it much easier to decide what is best for you. You're then able to make decisions that are aligned to your values and missions.

When you're clear on your core desire feelings, you become an "intentional creator" of your life as Danielle puts it. When you focus on your core desires, you'll be able to recognize when you're not feeling it.

We can't control what happens, but we can control our reaction and experience to what happens. Focusing on your core desires allows you in those moments to take back your control and ask yourself; "what can I do to generate my core desire feelings"?

The more personal and strong your why is and the feelings behind it, the more power it'll have to help you overcome obstacles that you'll face.

Higher Purpose

When you begin to take the steps to achieving your goals, it's important to also keep in mind the higher purpose of your aspirations. What I mean by this is understanding the bigger impact of yours goals. I just shared about the importance of uncovering your core desire feelings for your goals. Now I'm asking you to discover the impact your goals will have to the people around you. If you want more abundance and wealth, what impact will it have on your family, friends and causes you care about? Chances are the more wealth and abundance you have and experience the more you'll share with these people. When you see it from this perspective you're able to see that it's about much more than just you (and your goals).

Let your goals be aligned to a greater good. It isn't enough for it to be purely materialistic because it won't have enough power to sustain your efforts in the face of difficulty. Now I'm not saying it's not appropriate to have materialistic pursuits, you absolutely can! However, the more your goals enrich the lives of others; it feels more purposeful and has the power to sustain your efforts while allowing you to feel fulfilled in the process of achieving it.

Let your 'whys' and goals feel powerful and intimate. More money can mean freedom to spend more time with your family and help those closest to you. Just like the "why" to lose weight for better health, disease prevention, longevity to keep up with your kids and future grandkids, is more powerful than looking hot in a bikini for your next trip. Again, there's nothing wrong with wanting to look hot in a bikini for a trip but that won't sustain your efforts to work out consistently and make better food choices. That'll only make you choose short cuts and not make sound decisions for your health. Be clear and unapologetic about your why because that is a clear indication that you know you're worthy of it. This level of worthiness raises your vibrations to be in alignment with what you desire. When you desire something yet feel bad or guilty for wanting it, you send God/Universe mix messages.

The feeling of guilt is a negative low-level energy that's not aligned with the good you wish to bring into your life. It blocks the manifestation of your goals. When you see your goals as benefitting the whole, the sense of guilt is diminished

I remember early on when I was focused on building my career and creating more wealth, one of my measures of wealth and focus was buying a BMW 328 xi. Now, I'm not a car person, nor do I know what that car was about, but I remember seeing the car and thinking to myself, "now this represents wealth and being rich." I remember telling one of my good friends, and had the image of it cut out to put on my vision board. Although it felt cool thinking about how I would look driving that car, it was not intimate and strong enough. It didn't strike an emotional chord with me, nor was it enough to make me take risks needed to achieve the level of wealth I wanted at the time.

Now, my desire for wealth in order to support my mother, and see her relaxing, enjoying life and not worried about money, filled my heart with so much joy! It drove and motivated me.

Later as I became a mom for the first time, I had this overwhelming need to serve in a greater way. To help others achieve their dreams. In order to do that, I had to achieve mine and lead by example. The thought of my mother, serving others to make a better world for my kids, was a drive that was so strong! Stronger than what a BMW, no matter how great I may have looked in it, could have given me. When roadblocks and delays came my way, the vision of giving my mom that sense of freedom and my children growing up in a better world provided enough of the energy and drive I needed to keep going beyond my setbacks. I have yet to retire my mom, but the idea drives me to this day!

Tools to Stir your Imagination

I want to spend a little bit of time here to share some great tools that will really help ignite your imagination and use it bring you closer to your goals. Many of the techniques I'll share, you may have heard already, and possibly have done yourself. However, if you've yet to manifest your biggest desires utilizing these techniques, then you may have missed an important component that will help you have better results than you previously had.

Journaling

The first time I came across the concept of journaling I believe was when I embarked on my coaching career. The program I took to become certified taught about writing out your dream day. I was to write it out in great detail, adding juicy details and really seeing and tasting it as I wrote. I loved this exercise (so much) that I also included it in my programs.

This concept was taken further when I read Jack Canfield's, *Success Principals*. In the book, he shared a story about a lady who recently started a job in a bank. She was told that if their sales team didn't turn things around fast and generate large sales, the whole team would lose their jobs.

Now they tried all the different sales strategies taught to them without success. It did not work for her team. Because the traditional sales 'tactic' was not working for them, she decided to try out the journal technique that she heard about, where you take a journal and write a page of what you wanted to have as if you already had it. The theory was, by the time you got to the end, you'd have what you wanted.

The book went on to say how she didn't have a lot of time, so she got the smallest book she could find that was about 25 pages and started the process. She wrote about her prospects loving her products and how they couldn't wait to use it. She detailed the emotions and connections she'd have with these prospects as well.

Long story short, as she continued with this method, in addition to following intuitive guidance that was prompted, a miraculous, coincidental experience occurred. She met someone who needed her products in a big way and wanted it implemented in his company right away, giving her the success that she wanted and wrote about in her journal.

This led me to do the same. I found a small and pretty book, and started writing out my dream life scenario. I used a small book, and then graduated to another prettier book that was bigger that I could use to do more activities to help imprint my consciousness with the goals that I wanted to achieve.

Something I did with this new book was to not only write out what I wanted to have and achieve, but I also used it to write out my affirmations in order to impress it into my subconscious mind. We've been programmed for many years in beliefs that do not serve us, and ones that hold us back. Exercises like this allow you to start changing these impressions and training your mind to see things as you'd like them to be. You start to re-program it to think that your goals are no longer an aspiration, but have been fulfilled.

Now, when you try this exercise, I don't want it to be something you feel you need to do and it becomes a chore. If this is the case, please do not do it. This exercise is supposed to be fun and feel good to you. It should stir your imagination to believe in the possibilities of your dreams.

The reason why I also write out my affirmations is due to something I picked up from one of my mentors, Marilyn Jenett, who was a student of the great Dr. Joseph Murphy, whose book, *The Power of the Subconscious Mind,* is a must-read. Both Marilyn and Dr. Murphy, taught their students to write out their affirmations daily by hand 25 times.

This may seem excessive to some, but there's a link between writing something by hand and it having a greater impact on your mind. Your mind is better able to receive and retain the information you're writing, consequently having a greater impression.

When you journal daily, you ignite your imagination, and are able to get involved in the detail. Remember your mind does not know if you're imagining or if it's happening in real life. This helps you to see your desires vividly and convince your mind that you're already living and achieving what you want. You're living from the end and acting 'as if' on paper.

If I haven't' yet convinced you to start writing down what you want and your affirmations, it's also been shown that the act of writing triggers cells of the brain called the reticular activating system (RAS). Everything your brain needs to process information is filtered through the reticular activating system and distinguishes between urgent and non-urgent information. It gives more importance to things you're actively focused on. Your brain begins to work actively and alerts you to things that are consistent to what you've written.

Vision Boards

Vision boards are something most people are familiar with, and very simple to do. Basically you grab a bunch of magazines, scissors, glue and a large board and get to work! What you want to do is cut out images and words of what it is you want to have, be and achieve. Use words and images that evoke strong emotions for you.

If it's money you want, you can cut and paste images of money, but you want to go even further. What does having that money mean to you? Why do you want it? Most people want it for more security and freedom, and if that's the case, cut and paste pictures that represent freedom and security on your board because that's the core and what you're truly after. Look to your core desire feelings and cut out words and images that match them.

There are countless stories of people who have used the power of a vision board to manifest their dreams. I have also done the same! Prior to having my second child and still working in a corporate environment, I had pictures of a family of four and working from home. I am blessed to have both materialize in my life.

I also recently read about the amazing story shared by Oprah Winfrey about how in the morning of the US Presidential election on November 4, 2008, she was speaking to Michelle Obama, Caroline Kennedy, and Maria Shriver at a big rally in California. At the end of the rally, Michelle Obama said, "I want you to leave here and envision Barack Obama taking the oath of office." Oprah went home and created her first vision board and put Barack's picture on it and the dress she wanted to wear to the inauguration.

Now you may argue that he would have won regardless, but I remember the powerful vision many people held for Barack to be president. I sure did and I'm Canadian!

It's such an amazing thing that vision boards are becoming a norm and even many celebrities speaking about how they've used it to make their dreams a reality. From the story shared by John Assaraf in The Secret, where he had a picture of a home in his vision board and years later found himself living in the exact same house to other famous stories from Steve Harvey, Jim Carrey, Ellen DeGeneres and more.

I love the quote from Lucinda Cross, who credits the power of a vision board for transforming her life from being in prison as a young college student, to becoming a successful entrepreneur, best selling author, speaker and life coach. She says, "Whether you look at it (vision board) from a spiritual or scientific aspect, this world is a huge vision board. Everything that's here is because it started as an image someone had in their mind. You want to call it a blueprint, or a business plan? Fine. But first, they had to think about it and draft it. So a vision board? It's like selling our own ideas to ourselves."

Creative Visualization

I absolutely adore creative visualization. Visualization is a powerful exercise that gets you into the detail of what it is you want to achieve. It's a powerful step that bridges the gap to your dreams and opens the floodgates for opportunities to its attainment.

I first heard of creative visualization through one of my spiritual teachers, Gabrielle Bernstein. She shared the classic book, *Creative Visualization*, by Shakti Gawain, as one she reads periodically and practices on a regular basis. I had to check out this process because I've studied the power of visualization before and believed in the process and I wanted to learn more. I quickly got my hands on the book and loved the great and simply technique shared.

Based on *Creative Visualization* by Shakti Gawain, the steps are as follows:

Step 1. Set your goal.

Decide on what you want. What do you want to achieve, have and be? What's your aspiration? It can be anything you want, but make the decision on what it is you want. To start, you may choose something that's not as grand which I'll speak about a little later, and with practise you can move on to bigger things.

Step 2. Create a clear idea or picture.

This is where you ignite your imagination. Create a mental picture or feeling of what you want or situation exactly as you want it. Think from the end and see and feel it as if it's already been accomplished in as much detail as possible.

Step 3. Focus on it often.

Think about your idea and mental picture often. You can sit in the vision of what you want to create in quiet meditation time, and also throughout your day. Call it up as you go about your day in a nice and relaxed way. In the book she states to ensure you do not feel like you're 'striving too hard for it.' The striving to hard puts excessive amount of energy into it, which hurts the process. If you do it in meditative practice end it with: "This or something better."

Step 4. Give it positive energy.

When you think and focus on your goals, be positive and encouraged as if it already exists. Suspend any disbelief and put complete trust in it and revel in the joy of it.

What I love about this technique is that you do it in

short periods. You do not have to spend 10-20 minutes a day in creative visualization. All you need to do is commit to only a couple of minutes throughout your day to change your life.

As in the teachings of Abraham-Hicks, if you can hold a thought for 17 seconds without contradicting it (doubt, fear, negative believes etc.), you activate the Law of Attraction. If you can remain in this state of pure focus of your desire for 68 seconds, the manifestation of your desire begins to take shape. They even go on to say that 17 seconds of pure positive vibration (without any contradicting thoughts) is equal to 2000 action hours!

As you can see, it's not necessary that you devote a lot of time to it, but a little goes a long way. However, it's important that throughout your day, let yourself daydream of your goals and focus on the feelings that you'd have once it's already achieved.

Don't focus on how it will come about. Just stay focused on what you want to achieve and see yourself feeling the emotions that you'll feel once you've crossed the bridge to your goals. This is the power that will help you manifest your dreams.

Guided Visualization

Similar to creative visualization is guided visualization, which is listening to someone (or your own recording) guide you through the visualization. You can find many guided visualizations online using a simple google search on all kinds of topics. My favourite are ones from Abraham-Hicks. I also have one that I created that's part of my Mind Money Miracle online program.

Guided visualizations take you through a journey where you visualize your dream results. I love the ones with beautiful background music that really set the stage for you to step into your dream state.

The visualization that I created for my program is focused on financial abundance. I take you through several affirmations to help you change your limiting programs around money. It's full of affirmations and mantras, and set in beautiful background music so your conscious mind can relax and the affirmations and mantras I provide sink into your subconscious mind.

A powerful thing to do is to record the guided visualization in your own voice and listen to it. Your voice is more recognizable to you and will impact your mind.

Living your Imagination

As you start to live in your imagination, see yourself consistently being and having what it is you want. This goes beyond the two minutes of daily visualization I just wrote about. Get in the habit of seeing yourself already achieving your goals. Imagine that the bridge between your goals has been crossed and the fulfillment of your desires is now complete.

Start *being* the person who's already achieved your goal. This is all about embodying your goal and feeling giddy inside as if it's already happened, because truly, it has. Remember I started with the concept of a parallel universe. The person you wish to become is already present, waiting to materialize into form, so trust in your visions and celebrate it NOW! When you visualize you are directing and setting your outcome. The energy in which you live in is creating your future, so it's important to *be* the energy you want to create!

Stop for a second and picture what you'd do and feel if you've already achieved your goal. See yourself now living your dream lifestyle. What would it look and feel like? Who are you with? What are you wearing? Engage all your senses. See this picture throughout your day and feel good in your body about it. This is the *mind body spirit connection*. Feel it in your body!

If I still haven't convinced you how powerful visualization and imaging your desired future can be, I'd like to refer you to the famous experiment conducted by Australian Psychologist Alan Richardson. Alan chose three groups of students at random. He divided them into three groups and tested their ability to make free throws (shooting from the foul line into the basketball net).

One group was made to practice for 20 minutes every day. The other group was not allowed to practice, but for 20 minutes visualized themselves making free throws. The last group was not to practice nor visualize.

At the end of the study the results were amazing. The group that practiced daily improved their shots by 24%. The group that did not practice nor visualized, as expected did not have much improvements. However, the group that only visualized improved their shooting by 23%! This was almost the same percentage improvement by those that physically practiced. Now, I would've loved to see the percentage improvement that would have happened if they incorporated daily practice AND visualization, but it goes to show the remarkable results you can get with visualization.

Another example is Award Winning actor Will Smith. He attributes the Law of Attraction, visualization and positive thinking to his success. In Will's own words, "In my mind, I've always been an A-list Hollywood superstar. Y'all just didn't know yet". The late, great boxing legend Muhammad Ali has always said to have seen himself winning before the actual fight took place. Such is the power of using your imagination to manifest your dreams.

There's also the famous story of actor Jim Carrey, writing himself a 10 million dollar cheque for 'acting services rendered', when he was a struggling actor. He dated it Thanksgiving 1995, and put it in his wallet. And just before Thanksgiving 1995, was when he found out he was going to be earning 10 million dollars for the movie Dumb and Dumber.

Jim Carrey also employed visualization to achieve his goals. He would visualize himself being a sought after actor, and things that he wanted coming to him. It would make him feel better just thinking about it and he would tell himself that he indeed had these things. He may not have a hold on it just yet, but that it was out there for him.

There are many examples that go beyond actors and athletes. People have employed the power of their imagination to build successful businesses, improve their health, and better their relationships and more. They first saw it in their minds, took action and achieved success. No matter how far away your dreams may seem to you, they can become closer to manifesting when you're able to first see and visualize it.

Crawl Walk Run

Sometimes dreaming big may present some baggage for you especially if you've built a lot of blocks around why you can't have what it is you want. If this is the case for you, I want to introduce you to what I call the *Crawl Walk Run* strategy.

This is something I do a lot with my one on one clients in both personal and business coaching. This is based on the concept of gradually getting to your goals. Now, this does not mean you can't have quantum shifts and jump; you absolutely can. However, there are people for whom the big picture is just too scary to face and they need to gradually get there.

If this sounds like you, just build on your goals. So, using the example I gave earlier about earning $25,000 a month, if this feels too big for you, then the $25,000 can be your 'run' goal.

You can then break it down to $15,000 being your walk goal and then $8000 being your crawl goal. Now making $8000 can be a big stretch for you especially if you're coming from nothing, but the crawl should still be something that stretches you and you feel excited about. At the same time feeling manageable and doable for you.

When you then focus on the $8000 goal and what it would mean to your family and business, it's less scary. You don't have to deal with the anxiety that comes from looking at the $25,000 goal. The great thing with this method is that once you've achieved the $8000 goal, your walk goal of $15,000 will seem more achievable. When you finally reach the $25,000 mark, you'll confidently increase the number again and again!

Expectation

I want to share a little about expectations. This is something I've read in many places where people are taught to give up expectations as a way to not feel pain and hurt. I have a complete different take on it. I feel it's important to have expectations. I expect to have my goals come true and for my greatest aspirations to manifest. This is something I strongly believe in because we tend to get what we expect to get.

The issue I see with expectation is when people get attached to it. It's a fine line I know, but what has worked for me is to have expectations however I'm detached from them. This means that I expect to have my goals come about, but I'm not attached to the form it takes.

The one area I feel you have to release expectations is when it involves others. As you may know, you can't control anyone nor expect him or her to behave a certain way. People have their own free will and to impose upon that goes against their need to choose for themselves. When you release your expectations of others that is when you let go of the pain that comes along when someone does not comply to what your expectations are of them.

However, when it comes to expecting your goals to materialize, by all means please have expectations and open your heart to receive it. Train your brain to expect what you want to happen. Assume that your aspirations are now fulfilled and you're now living it. This is how change and manifestations happen. You'll receive what you prepare and expect to get. Expect the outcomes that you desire and you will start seeing them. Wake up every morning stating "something great is going to happen to me today!" Feel the excitement of something great happening to you or receiving great news about something that you want. Really feel it. It only takes a few seconds and has the capacity to turn your day and life around!

I want to end this chapter quoting an email I got from *Notes from the Universe,* which is a daily email I receive from Mike Dooley over at tut.com. Mike is one of the teachers featured in The Secret and his emails are so personalized and filled with insights and humour. It has become something I look forward to every morning. There was a message I got one day, which really brings home the importance of using your imagination to lead you to your dream.

"Uchechi, it is easy. Just once a day, imagine the life you dream of. Believe that it can be yours in this world of magic and miracles. Choose to live as if you know of its inevitable manifestation. Don't compromise. Don't worry. Don't look for results. And as surely as spirit crafts one moment after another, so too will it fuse together the life you now lead with the life of your dreams as if they were two pieces of a jigsaw puzzle, destined to become one.

This alone determines what's "meant to be."

Tallyho,

The Universe"

CHAPTER 6

Clearing Space and Overcoming Resistance

"When we create space in our lives, we make way
for the hands of the Divine to fill it with those
things our hearts have long been asking for."
~ Chris Assaad

I want to take time now to share an important principal to incorporate in order to see the manifestation of your dreams. This is all about welcoming your dreams and making space for it.

The concept of clearing space (also known as releasing) is based on the fact that you have to first release the old, in order to receive something new into your life. You have to decide and let it go and remove it from your consciousness.

This means to de-clutter and clear space physically, mentally and emotionally, to allow the new desire to come into your life.

I like to use the example of your hands. So if you're holding onto something, your hands are closed and shut right? If I was to give you something new, and you wanted to take hold of and receive it, you'll need to open up your hands right? And if you did open your hands and the old thing was there, to grasp the new, you would need to let it go to have space in your hands to receive. Well, that is exactly how it works with your life too.

How many times have you held onto things, people, situations, and circumstances you did not want? You keep holding on, regardless of the pain it's causing you. This is because although what you're holding onto is causing you pain, the fear of the unknown is equally if not more painful for you, thus keeping you stuck.

Furthermore, your subconscious mind loves to keep you in what is known and comfortable, so you'll start seeing and experiencing situations to keep you in your comfort zone.

When you don't have what you desire even though you may be doing the work and aligning yourself to your goals, it could be that you're still holding onto something that is inconsistent with what you want to bring into your life. You have yet to let it go.

How many times have you held onto something, all the while hoping for something different? A great example is in relationships. I've seen this so many times, and myself included. You want to be in a loving and committed relationship however, you're still holding onto your ex who you know will never commit to you. You pine for him or her and drop all your plans whenever they ask. Because you haven't released this past relationship, you're preventing someone new from coming into your life. It will be very difficult for you to bring in that new committed relationship into your life, no matter how much you visualize and affirm it.

I'll use an example in my own life. There was someone I cared deeply for. He was a good friend and I wanted more, but unfortunately, he preferred to stay friends (don't you just hate when that happens?!). I kept hanging onto the hope that he would one day see just how perfect we were for each other... but it didn't happen. So finally, I made the decision that I wanted someone who wanted more from me.

It was when I made the decision that I met someone who I was involved with for many years. The funny part about this situation was that this person I became involved with said he met me at a party previously. I had no recollection of him whatsoever, as it was during the time that I was emotionally involved with my friend. He said he was there, met me and I was oblivious to it. I see now that because I was holding on to someone else emotionally, I wasn't able to 'see' him. Now this relationship did not work out at the end, but he became a dear friend and served as a great example of how we can miss out, when we refuse to let go.

Another reason creating space is a requirement to receive something new is because, "nature abhors a vacuum". This means that when an empty space is created, nature rushes in and fills it up with something new. So, you must create an empty space by releasing in order to have that new desire be welcomed into your life.

I do want to advise though, that once you fully commit to clearing space, you may experience some shadows. These are things that show up for you to deal with. Clearing space calls forth all the 'baggage' that needs to be cleaned up to come forth. It may mean dealing with a past relationship, or going through your home and de-cluttering. You'll come across some resistance as you start clearing, but this is just a part of the process and an opportunity to release them. When you release negative energy, it is then that you can experience the change you want.

Many people struggle with letting things go in order to clear space, so I am going to take the opportunity now to share some great tools that have helped me and countless of others clear space and deal with the resistance that comes up as a result.

Forgiveness

Forgiveness is the ultimate way to clear space in your life. Think about it, when you're holding onto resentment, anger, and holding a grudge, it feels tight and restricting. It keeps you out of flow. As you learnt through the Law of Attraction and Law of Cause and Effect, this will only bring you more of the same (feeling of tightness and restriction).

The feeling that comes from anger and resentment are low-level frequencies that put you out of alignment to receive the good that you want into your life.

People often struggle with forgiveness because they think they are in some way condoning the situation, event or person, but that's farther from the truth. Remember forgiveness is not about the other person, but rather about releasing the hold the pain has on *your* life. You're freeing yourself from it, and not allowing it to take space in your life.

Buddha reminded us of this when he said, "Holding onto anger is like drinking poison and expecting the other person to die." Resentment and anger act like poison that harms only you, by keeping you connected to the situation, person and event. When you allow yourself to forgive you have the ability to break the bond it has on your life. You become free from the toxic feelings in exchange for peace.

Financial struggles are also linked to resentments and grievances. Think about the energy associated with resentment. It feels dark, heavy and does not feel good. At some level you feel that you are 'owed' something, and guess what happens? Your subconscious mind picks up on the energy of 'owed'. You feel that someone did you wrong and 'owes' you an apology. Your focus and attention then goes to how someone *owes* you an apology, you did not get. These little details are picked up by the subconscious mind and manifests in different areas of our life, one of which can be your finances. You may find yourself in a position where you owe money to other people, and have outstanding bills to pay.

If we look at this from a Law of Attraction perspective, you focused and impressed your mind with owing; resulting in events and situations where owing to others came into your awareness, because you became a vibrational match to it. See how that works?

Forgive anyone who you feel has contributed to any problems or pain that is going on in your life, even if they've yet to give you the apology you feel they 'owe' you. Don't forget to add yourself to the list. Sometimes, we place more blame and guilt on ourselves than others. Forgive yourself for any part you feel you played in the situation you now face that you don't want, or for the fact that you feel you haven't been able to fulfill your greatest aspirations.

I've heard it numerous times, 'you can only feel one emotion at any one time' and when you're consumed with anger and resentment, there's no room for love and abundance.

I want to share a powerful forgiveness exercise that can help you move past resistance you may have to it.

Ho'oponopono

Ho'oponopono is a gentle Hawaiian practice of reconciliation and forgiveness. It literally means to 'make right'. It's a simple practice that's highly effective. I first heard of Ho'oponopono, from Money Mindset Mentor, Denise Duffield-Thomas.

I later researched it farther and learnt just how powerful and amazing this practice is through another teacher of mine, Joe Vitale from the hit movie *The Secret*.

Joe's teaching on this remarkable practice is the most complete work that I've found that really explains the benefits of it. I highly recommend you read his book, *Zero Limits*, which explains how he came across this mysterious practice, and the profound results it can have on clearing you from past pain, hurt and resentment, and open you to the flow of more abundance and joy.

In *Zero Limits*, Vitale shares how he came across a mysterious therapist Dr. Ihaleakala Hew Len. He heard of a therapist that healed a whole ward of criminally insane patients without seeing them. The therapist healed them through the practice Self I-Dentity through Ho'oponopono (SITH).

Dr. Hew Len reviewed each of the patient's files

and healed them simply by healing himself! The results were astonishing. Dr. Hew Len explained that because those patients were in his life, he took responsibility for healing parts of him that created them being there. As he worked on himself, his patients began to heal. According to him, the patient's behaviour was due to their past programs and memories, and in order to heal them he had to remove the memories by 'cleaning' it, which he did through himself.

The patients in the ward after a few months did not need to be shackled, and were allowed to freely walk around the ward. Some that were heavily medicated got off their medication. Even those that were not given a chance of being released were freed. The ward as a result had more staff than they needed because patients were being released and ended up closing.

I know this sounds surreal and bizarre, but the research and results are outstanding. When I started to first research this technique, I thought if he could have such amazing results with these types of patients, the possibilities are endless.

Personally when I do this practice, I feel calmer, my relationships seem to flow smoother, and I'm just happier. As you know, the happiness expands and gets bigger and stronger.

The foundation of this practice is about taking responsibility. Whatever has shown up for you and is now in your awareness is a projection of what is happening inside of you. It's based on your beliefs and memories. This may be difficult to acknowledge, but at the same token, because you're now taking responsibility means you have the power to clean, clear and transform it. Just like I've been sharing in this book, to heal anything outside of you requires you healing what's inside.

The process of Ho'oponopono is to go through each person, situation, or thing that causes you pain and feel your emotions. Think of things that you're still holding onto. Let any feelings or emotions connected with each one come up for you. Don't try to resist it. Next you say (out loud or in your head) the following statement:

"I love you."
"I'm sorry."
"Please forgive me."
"Thank you."

That's it, quick and simple. It doesn't matter if you're looking to forgive someone or yourself, you use the same mantra for all situations. As Joe teaches, "the words are a way of clearing energy for the person saying the mantra. No matter who was involved or what happened, this will remove the associated energies on your end, and is a way of saying to the Universe, 'I no longer allow these dark and heavy energies to live in my body, mind and spirit.'"

I've been asked by those I've taught this practice to, who they should be directing the mantra too, and it's taught that you simply direct it to Source/God. You don't have to have someone present in order to experience it, simply say the mantras without directing it to anyone or direct the energy to Source/Universe.

I've read countless posts and articles about the healing power of this practice and it's something I've done in my own life too that's given me a sense of peace and calm, as well to those whom I've shared it with.

Each mantra from Ho'oponopono is important because it starts with taking responsibility for all that's showed up for you.

I'm Sorry ~ When you say, 'I'm sorry, you're taking full responsibility of whatever it is that is happening around you with the understanding that it's a projection of what is happening within you. Whatever is showing up is also based on past memories that continue to re-create themselves over and over again. They are the same lessons showing up which you created and are now taking full responsibility for.

Please forgive me ~ When you say, 'please forgive me', it's not about guilt nor blame. It's not that you necessarily did anything wrong, but rather about acknowledging that whatever is happening is caused by old memories (programs/stories) repeating in your life in a different ways. You are the common denominator and thus the issues stem from within you. Asking for forgiveness, is asking that Spirit clear the memories from you and all the way through to your past and ancestors. This is what the forgiveness is about, 'clearing' the memories and energies within you that are causing the situation.

Thank you ~ this mantra is about showing gratitude that Spirit takes care of you and has indeed cleared the past memories that are causing the unwanted experience in your life. You are acknowledging that it is a done deal and giving gratitude for your healing.

I love you ~ is there any greater power and emotion than love? I personally don't think so. Love has the ability to transmute anything undesired and turn it into miracles. This is what you're acknowledging when you say this mantra.

With Ho'oponopono, you use each conscious moment to clean your energy instead of being consumed with old and past memories replaying itself in the present moment.

De-Clutter your Surrounding

Another clearing technique to make space for new desires to feel welcomed is to physically de-clutter your surrounding. Look throughout your home and remove things that don't feel prosperous nor abundant- things that the person you wish to become would not want in their home. Surround yourself with things and people that support you and make you feel good. The energy that comes from that elevates you and puts you in the right frequency to match what you wish to have.

Don't forget your workspace, email inbox, closets, cupboards, etc. when de-cluttering. When you clear your physical space of clutter, you eliminate stale energy in your surroundings. By cleaning out old clutter from your space, you trigger the process of receiving new things into your life. You open up the flow and make room to receive new things into your life.

De-cluttering your physical surroundings also includes those you choose to spend most of your time with. So much has been said with respect to the impact of the company we keep. The people we choose to spend the majority of our time with have a huge influence on who we'll be and what we'll accomplish in our life. Tony Robbins says; "Who you spend time with is who you become! Change your life by consciously choosing to surround yourself with people with higher standards!" Some people are easier to avoid than others, as there are times when these people are close to you and it is very difficult to avoid them, however you can definitely start to minimize the time you spend with them and the effects they have on you.

As cliché as this may sound, prayer is a great tool to help reduce the energetic impact of those you must spend time with. If the difficult person is a family member; pray for them. If it's a boss that you must deal with everyday; pray for him or her. If it's an important client that is critical to your business growth and success; pray for them. I truly believe that every prayer is answered. It may come in the form of the person becoming more positive and easier to get along with, or simply be that you change your perception of the situation and see it differently, and with more compassion.

The Power of your Tribe

Having a strong and supportive community is a great way to help you live the best version of yourself, and move past resistance. Support Community is one of the three keys Master Life Coach Mark Fournier writes about in his Life Mastery program that I've mentioned before. You need the support of a community in order to accomplish your goals. No one has ever accomplished anything great on their own. People along the way have directly or indirectly helped them achieve their goals. It's important to surround yourself with people who are able to help you maintain a positive perspective, support you and truly wish for you to succeed.

I've personally made changes in the past, when I saw myself being pulled down by people around me. When I reviewed and took inventory of the negative impact it had on me; which affected my interaction with my family, it was at that point that I could no longer tolerate the negative energy. My sense of well-being and positive outlook was worth more to me. Your future success and quality of life depends on the energy of those you choose to surround yourself with.

Having mentors is another great way to get support. This is especially important for business and career development. I love connecting with others, especially those in positions that I aspire to. It's important to learn from these people. Unfortunately, many times we allow ourselves to be influenced by those who are controlled by their fears. We take advice from those that are struggling in areas where we wish to thrive. Re-examine those that you take advice from. Do they have the type of life you want? Do they have missions and values you respect? Be conscious of those you associate with and see if they fuel and expand your energy or drain it. Start to eliminate those that are draining your energy and fill yourself with those who uplift you!

Overcoming Resistance

When you make a decision to boldly go after your goals and dreams, a strange thing tends to happen. You come up with resistance. When you look at it through the lens of your conditioned mind, you know it is a signal being sent to your brain that you are no longer safe. If you're aspiring to something you've never done before, and it's inconsistent with your current way of being, it will call up different things for you.

It's been referred to, as the Universe calling up things in your life so you can identify what needs clearing, in order to make room for you to receive what you wish for. This resistance can often look like set-backs and can feel painful. It's at this time that you must fix your eyes on your goals and maintain the frequency of it, regardless of what shows up for you.

It reminds me of one of my favourite metaphysical teacher and author, Florence Scovel Shinn, wrote in her classic book *The Game of Life and How to Play It*. She wrote, 'Every great work, every big accomplishment, has been brought into manifestation through holding to the vision, and often just before the big achievement, comes apparent failure and discouragement.'

Sometimes the resistance may show up as the work being 'too difficult' or all of a sudden, the very thing you were all excited to do, is no longer exciting and you feel that you want to quit. Or it may not feel as fun as you thought it would.

This is something I see often, especially when I work and meet with other business owners. There is always the first rush of excitement when the desire is first felt, and you start dreaming and thinking of all the possibilities. You then start of to take steps to make it happen, and like I just mentioned, the steps may be outside of your comfort zone. This leads many people to doubt their action and goals and look to things that feel better at the moment, instead of continuing with the goal they've set for themselves.

It is difficult to remain focused on your goals during this time of resistance and that's when the following tools can be useful to get you through this difficult period.

EFT

EFT is a tool I love and share with my clients. It's noninvasive and can be done whenever you're feeling fearful, anxious and full of resistance.

EFT stands for Emotional Freedom Technique and also known as tapping. It's a powerful tool to use to reduce anxiety and emotional build-ups that tend to show up, every time you try to expand and reach beyond your comfort zone.

This powerful practice combines tapping energy meridians on your body and saying positive affirmation to help you clear emotional blocks from your body. While you are tapping on the key points around your face and body, you say the mantra: "Even though I have this fear (state the particular fear or resistance you're experiencing), I deeply and completely love and accept myself."

When practicing and doing the tapping, the mantra

is important because, you're saying no matter what; you deeply and completely love and accept yourself. Because if you don't love and accept yourself then you're not going to believe you are worthy to fulfill your dreams. When you don't believe you're worthy, you end up sabotaging your efforts and as a result remain stuck. This practice allows you to first acknowledge your negative emotions, and then you release them so they don't block you from receiving your desires.

EFT, helps you take control of your emotions immediately. I often find that one round of tapping helps me reduce the anxiety I may be feeling.

A technique I also like to do is to tap as I read and say my affirmations and mantras, especially as I sense that my subconscious mind does not buy into it and resisting it. It helps reduce the anxiety that surfaced. Again it's simple, yet powerful and can give you immediate results.

I highly suggest you research further into EFT, if this is your first time hearing about it, as it can provide you with amazing results. There are numerous videos on the Internet that can be a great resource for you. My favourites are from Brad Yates, an EFT expert. Nick and Jessica Ortner from *The Tapping Solution* are great resources as well.

CHAPTER 7

Living in Alignment

"Let your alignment with Well-Being be first and foremost and let everything else be secondary. And not only will you have an eternally joyous journey, but everything you have ever imagined will flow effortlessly into your experience. There is nothing you cannot be, do or have - but your dominant intent is to be JOYFUL."
~Abraham-Hicks

As the quote above demonstrates, one of the fastest ways to go from aspiring to achieving something is to be in alignment. To be honest, most of the content of this book consists of ways to get in alignment and a vibrational match to what you want.

When you're in the flow and feel aligned, you're in the best position to easily and quickly turn any aspiration into fulfillment. Success will chase you when you stay aligned, on purpose and committed to your vision. When you're living in alignment, you give up the reasons why you can't have what you want and focus on why you can. When you focus on your aspirations without doubt about achieving it, you then have the power to create extraordinary results.

It's important to take time each day to dedicate to some form of an alignment practice. The morning is the best time, as it helps set the stage for the rest of your day. I know many of you will resist this as you may say mornings are already busy enough and there is *no way* you can cram in yet another activity in your morning routine. If this is what you're thinking, I'd love to share something Tony Robbins said when he was on Super Soul Sunday. He said, "If you don't have ten minutes, then you don't have a life." What he means by this is if you're unwilling to carve out just ten minutes in your twenty-four hour day to devote to yourself and cultivating habits that will bring you ultimate joy and happiness, then you'd be unable to live a quality life.

Tony shared something he calls 'priming', which to me is the same as getting yourself in alignment before starting your day. What he does is as follows:

- Spend three minutes in absolute gratitude (you may want to use this time to write in your gratitude journal)
- Another three minutes sending love to everyone you can think of. This includes your colleagues, clients and wishing them success in their business as well.
- And the last three minutes in active visualization

You can use the same as Tony suggests or do a two-minute creative visualization as I've shared in this book.

If you're still reading this and not fully committed to dedicating this time, then I'd suggest that your desire is not yet strong enough and that you revisit your why and the higher purpose of your aspirations. Just 10-15 mins a day to make a difference in your life is worth it. You need to do this for you, because your visions and dreams are calling on you to do it!

Attitude of Gratitude

One of the best ways to be aligned to Source and a vibrational match to what you want is through gratitude.

You've probably heard it before and it won't be the last time that you'll hear it, but gratitude is truly a powerful way to live a miraculous and abundant life! When you appreciate what you have around you, regardless of what appears to be the absence of what you desire, it helps keep you in the flow to receive more. It also allows you to see things through an empowered lens and you become a happier person.

You need to be happy and grateful for what you already have before you can get more. There is always something to be grateful for in all circumstances. The energy of gratitude raises your vibrations and aligns your energy to attract more things in your life that you can be grateful for.

Even if you find yourself in circumstances where you feel a sense of lack and unhappiness, there is a seed of positivity in it. Remember the Law of Polarity? Everyone has a reason to be happy and something they can appreciate. It could be your children, family, friends or the fact that you are alive reading this. It could be that

Uchechi Ezurike-Bosse

you have a job to go to each and every day. Yes, it may not be your dream job, but be happy that you have a job that pays you a regular paycheck.

The greater your feeling of appreciation the less resistance you'll feel. You'll be on the frequency to be able to see and experience more things to feel grateful for. Now appreciation and gratitude can be a funny thing, as sometimes people start practicing it in order to get more. I admit I did this too because I heard just how powerful it was to achieve your goals. However, it never truly gave me the results I wanted because I was basing my gratitude practice on receiving rather than giving gratitude for what I already had in my life.

When I started to be truly grateful for things, I didn't have to necessarily write it down in my gratitude journal, although I think they're great for many reasons and one in which I'll explain further. But feeling grateful felt so darn good! I looked at my life with new awareness and I compared how amazing my life is versus others who don't have as much as me. This is called the Law of Relativity which states that things are neither good nor bad unless you relate them to something else. So when I started to do this comparison I saw how truly blessed I was and that made me feel amazing. Yes the physical manifestation of my desire was not yet visible to my human eye, but just the feeling that I emitted was the energy that was bringing them into my life even faster and all I did was feel the beauty and blessings of what I had in my life already.

Something that I learned from the works of Abraham-Hicks is that more you practice gratitude, the better you feel, and the better you feel the more you genuinely want to do it, and as a result of wanting to do it, the better you feel and it just continues to grow.

This is exactly what happened to me. I felt so freaking amazing that it was incredibly easy to see how truly amazing my life was. It got to the point that even without the physical manifestation of what I wanted, I still felt so good and joyous inside.

And you know what happened? It was then that opportunities started coming into my life, more clients that loved my work, more money and opportunities to share my work. As they came in, I kept giving thanks for them! This state is so powerful because it puts you in the state to receive. You *allow* the good you want to come into your life. You're not adding resistance, but rather opening up the channel for the flow of what you want to come into your life. When you ask and desire something, Source already answers your call.

I love how Abraham-Hicks also describes the act of appreciation. They write, "Every time you *appreciate* something, every time you *praise* something, every time you *feel good* about something, you are telling the Universe: 'More of this, please.'" Think about that for a second. So if you can look around to the things in your life to be grateful for, even though your goals have yet to manifest, you're telling the great power that created our world to give you more of it.

This is another reason, why I love doing gratitude intentions. This is something I learnt from The Secret Gratitude journal, which I use as my personal gratitude journal. This is a powerful tool to attract miracles into your life at a faster rate. Because your mind does not distinguish between what you're imagining and giving thanks to versus what is actually happening, I start giving thanks and appreciation for the things I want to manifest before it actually happens.

You might feel that this is lying to yourself, but remember, creation first happens in the invisible realm. The version of you actually fulfilling your goals *is* already occurring in another reality. The bridge to your dreams starts to be built, and change happens when you remain in a state of gratitude and hold the vision of it being a done deal!

Gratitude Journal

The Universe really does give you more to be thankful for once you appreciate what you currently have in your life. I personally keep a daily gratitude journal, which I learnt, from The Oprah Winfrey Show. It has become a great tool for me because as I go about my day, I look for things I can be thankful for and write about at the end of my day. This allows me to look for the good all around me instead of focusing on the bad. Another reason, I love my gratitude journal is that I have something to review during challenging times. For me, whenever I find myself in a negative place, I take out my gratitude journal and read past entries. It never fails to lift my spirits.

You come closer to your dreams and become a deliberate creator of your life, when you focus your awareness on all the blessings you already have in your life.

Who are you being?

When you're able to bring in a feeling of gratitude in your life, and focus on 'being' that which you wish to become, and feeling as though it's already a reality; that is when magic and miracles happen. Your 'beingness' is what you're attracting into your life, and it's the act or state of being.

Another teacher of mine, Christie Marie Sheldon, puts it this way, "What you hold dear to you, you re-energize. What you're experiencing is a reference point to what you're thinking. Only live the energy you wish to call into your life in the future."

So whatever energy you're emitting (remember Law of Vibration and Attraction) that is what you're calling into your life. Live from the state you wish to have and it will be brought onto you. As James Lane Allen has been quoted to say, 'We do not attract what we want, but what we are'. What this means, and what I've been trying to impress to you through this book is that you can only attract what you are being- what you're aligned with. We focus so much on what we should be doing versus just being what it is you want.

If you find yourself struggling through life, then there's a disconnect between who you're currently being and what it is you want to become.

Inspired Action

Taking inspired action is very important in manifesting your dreams. One of the things that was criticized about

Uchechi Ezurike-Bosse

the movie The Secret was that people felt it gave the false message that all you had to do was to ask, believe and sit by and receive. It's important to remember that as you start to align yourself with Universal energy, doors will open for you, however; you must take **action** in order to achieve and receive your goals. It would be nice for you to sit around and wait for someone to give you what you need, but that simply will not happen. You need to be an active participant in the creation process and that involves taking action on the guidance and prompts that's given.

Inspired action means you're taking action on intuitive guidance given to you. We always get this guidance anytime we start moving towards our goals. It's the subtle impulse, internal nudge or flash of idea that we get. It's your job to act on these impulses and follow the inspiration.

There are so many people who resist this and talk themselves out of making a move, or they use the common excuse that they're not ready! Taking a step, no matter how little, opens doors and gives you an opportunity to take another one. It also makes a statement to the Universe that you trust and are willing to do what is needed to get to your goals.

Please remember, "You can't do it wrong!" Every action you take gets you closer to your goal. It can show what works best for you, lead you to success, or show you what does not work so you can cross it off your list and look to another option. Either way, there are lessons to be learned, so don't be afraid to take action and make mistakes. Action leads to progress and opportunities to help you reach your goals.

102

As you continue to take inspired action, you remain connected and hear your Higher Self more and more. It's just like a muscle, the more you use it, the stronger it becomes. So learn to trust your intuition, listen and take action to the messages you receive.

Another thing with taking action is to take immediate action. Oftentimes, we wait on the messages we've received and before we know it, we've talked ourselves out of it before doing anything about it.

I'm reminded of Mel Robbins's *TedTalk* where she mentions her five-second rule. The five-second rule helps you take action when you don't want to. In Mel's own words, "If you have an impulse to act on a goal, you must physically move within five seconds or your brain will kill the idea."

This is something I know I've experienced in my life and I'm sure you have too. I remember being in a business meeting with senior leaders in my corporate days. There were issues being discussed and I remember thinking I had great insights to share and I wanted to raise my hand and speak. However, the fear came up: 'What if they think my idea sucked?' Then I thought maybe I'll wait until everyone has spoken. As always in a few moments, the inspiration to speak goes away and I never speak up.

How many times have you had an inspired idea and felt so aligned, however you stalled and waited? Next thing you know, as time went on the idea no longer felt great and you chalked it up to it being too risky. As a result, you never proceeded to what it was you wanted to do.

Sometimes, the answer or result to your needs may not come directly from the action you took, but from another means. Because you had faith and took action in some direction, the next step will show up for you; you'll gain more clarity.

An example of this was when I was feeling conflicted with my work. I wanted clarity on how I should work with my business clients by incorporating spiritual and mental strategies that I know are essential for major breakthroughs and transformation. For some reason I always separated the two. When I blogged and taught solely on personal and spiritual development, I also wanted to teach about marketing, wealth creation and business development. Conversely, when I taught and wrote about business development I longed for spiritual conversations and teachings.

I booked a session with a friend who is an intuitive healer and as soon as I booked my appointment, a level of clarity came to me. I did not have my session yet, however I felt much clearer. This was because I made a demonstration and took action to actually seek clarity by *booking* my appointment. My friend actually reminded of this when I mentioned to her how surprised I was to be feeling the fog being lifted days prior to us meeting! I definitely got more clarity from her, but it started to come through faster as a result in me taking some form of action.

Start before you're ready

One of my mentors, Marie Forleo, has a saying of 'start before you're ready'. At first blush, this may seem a little irresponsible or hasty, but I honestly believe that is one of the best things you can do to achieve your goals. Of course this does not apply to someone wanting to do something as technical as open-heart surgery, but I'm thinking you're not reading this book to learn that. You see, many people are always "waiting" for the perfect time to do this or that, but, the truth is, there'll never be a perfect time. There is always something you'll feel you must master or learn before you take the step, and if left until you felt ready, chances are; you'll never do it. I truly believe most of the advances we now enjoy would not have been made possible, had those responsible for the creation of them; waited until they felt ready to embark on their creation.

When my sister and I first launched our Wellness Centre, we definitely started before we felt ready. We only had enough money raised to simply open the doors. Now I definitely recommend having more cash flow and at least 6-8 months of operating income, but the thing is; we were able to get through it. We learnt many lessons and now have transitioned and grown both personally and professionally from the experience.

I've met many people with big plans and goals. They have an idea or areas of interest they want to pursue, but they sit on it, waiting for the "perfect time" and to feel ready. If they're honest with themselves, they'll recognize that their excuse for not starting goes back to big ole fear- fear of failure and fear of success. What would people think? How will I manage? Don't get me wrong, I'm big on planning, but I also feel taking ACTION, especially inspired action is the way to create the reality you want to live.

Another great thing Marie Forleo says is that

"Everything is figureoutable." Yes, I know, that's not a real word, but you get the point. There are solutions to every problem out there. It doesn't matter what it is you want to achieve. Chances are, someone else has already achieved it, so there's no need to reinvent the wheel. Look to those who have achieved what you want and learn from them. There's no shortage of information in this day and age, so use it to your advantage.

Meditation

Another technique I use to maintain alignment is through meditation. Now, I know for some people, just hearing or reading the word makes you tense up and dismiss it. You feel you're one of those people that are just not into meditation and your mind just jumps and gets into thinking mode every time you try to meditate.

There's no doubt that meditation is a great way to get connected and align with Source, in addition to a wide range of mental and emotional benefits. Personally I love guided meditation where I listen to someone's voice, guiding me into the 'space within.' However, this practice may not work for everyone. There are different ways to meditate and some may resonate more or less with you.

In the past, I've tried to get one of my sisters to meditate. I've bought her one of my favourite-guided meditations to try, but it was just not for her. However, after she brings my niece and nephew to daycare and school, she comes home to an empty house, and sits in silence and lets the quietness and calmness in her home at that time wash over her before she starts her day. In my opinion that is a form of meditation.

I've also used music as a type of meditation. I'll put on some of my favourite inspiring songs, close my eyes and let the words and sounds carry me into complete bliss. I sometimes tear up and allow myself to cry. In those moments, I feel so aligned and connected to my Source. I feel so inspired after my 'music meditation' that it feels like I can take on the world and accomplish just about anything. In that case, I didn't sit cross-legged and hum to any mantra, but in a sense, that stillness felt so amazing and I felt aligned.

If you feel that traditional meditation does not work for you, give some of these a try. My mother-in-law loves to knit and sometimes can sit for long duration and just drift away as she knits. You may feel the same when you run or when you practice yoga, or even adult colouring that has taken off in popularity nowadays. All these activities are helping you take your mind off of worry and into a space of doing something that feels good and blissful to you.

CHAPTER 8

Divine Guidance

"Every heart has a divine intelligence and natural
guidance system. With every prayer, every meditation
and every thought of love, we tune in to ours."
~Marianne Williamson

I want to get into a topic that is truly the foundation
of achieving anything your heart desires, and really one
that is near and dear to me. This, in my opinion is the
foundation for co-creating and without it, you'll be met
with more resistance and find yourself chasing something
that was not truly in your heart.

This foundation is all about allowing for divine
guidance. What does that mean you may be asking? Well,
for me, divine guidance is the inner spirit that we all have.
It's the spiritual guidance that created this expansive and
massive universe we all live in. We call it different names
and even find ourselves arguing over its true name, but
that name is never important. What is important is that it
exists, and supports and carries us to our goals.

As I look back on my journey and some of the things

I pursued, I can clearly see some events that people would consider 'failure' were actually the times when I pushed and 'worked hard'. Now I'm not saying working hard is not important, as there is a time and place for it. What I'm saying is that when I failed to incorporate and invite Spirit into my work as a co-creator, were the times I experienced massive setbacks. I failed to ask for guidance before taking action and making a decision. I failed to see that there was this spiritual guidance that wanted me to achieve my goals even more than I wanted it for myself, because this spirit experiences and lives life *through* me.

I also think that the times I 'failed' were because I needed to learn this lesson, just like my big launch failure. I was taught to let go control over the situation. This is something that was not easy for me to accept, as I tend to want to control and direct my efforts and life. Feeling out of control caused me anxiety and the act of letting go to be divinely guided at times seemed somewhat irresponsible. However, it turned out to be one of the best things I did for my dreams and myself.

A personal example of this is when my husband and I wanted to add to our family. I had the grand old plan that after our wedding, we would add to our family. I had it all planned out, and it became a top priority in my life. However, month after month, it did not happen and every month that went by and I did not conceive, I grew more frustrated and anxious!

I couldn't understand after setting the intention, visualizing and affirmations that I was not able to conceive. I grew more disappointed as the months went by and very impatient.

Luckily, I got to a point where I felt an intuitive reassurance that my desire will come to pass, but I needed to just "chill out!" I had this feeling of release and a knowing that it will happen and the *when* was not up to me. I promised myself to stop putting my life on hold and just go about my business until it happens.

I made plans to do things I put off doing including, the master cleanse which is something I've done periodically in the past.

I released the intention to God and knew that my pregnancy would happen and I just had to have faith, and stop obsessing and go about my normal every day life and stop planning things around when I would get pregnant.

And, guess what? Just when I made the promise to release and let go, was around the time I conceived! I ended up not doing the cleanse, because I was then pregnant, and the timing both personally and professionally turned out to be the best one for me.

To top all of this, when my husband went home to grab some stuff to bring back to the hospital after I gave birth to my daughter, he took a picture of my Abram-Hicks perpetual calendar that I keep on my desk. The following was the message of the day on May 6th, the day my daughter was born:

"All desires are answered; all requests are granted; and no one is left unanswered, unloved, or unfulfilled. When you stay aligned with your Energy Stream, you always win-and somebody else does not have to lose for you to win-there is always enough."

Allowing for Spiritual Support

Something I truly believe is that if we're able to connect with spirit, right from the start, a lot of pain and suffering experienced on our journey would be avoided. Sometimes, just like in my example, we are taught the lesson to lean on this infinite guidance that is here ready to provide us with everything we need to manifest our desires.

You've probably heard that we're 'spiritual beings having a human experience'. Many teachers have taught us this. We're spiritual beings that are connected to the Source that created us. Remember, at the start of the book when I spoke about how we had a spark of the creator within us? It comes full circle here.

The beautiful thing about coming into union with our spiritual guidance is the ability to know that we do not need to do it all. Quite frankly, we can never do it all alone. This is what my experience has taught me. The divine presence in us works with us for the manifestation of our dreams. Whether you believe this to be true or not, it's waiting for you, however it requires your involvement and for you to ask for help.

When I find myself feeling helpless about something or overwhelmed by a task or goal that I have for myself and doubting my ability to create, I remind myself about the power within me. It is the same power that created the vastness of our universe, parted water, moved mountains. Whenever I think about it in this context, it lights a fire within me and I can see how small my problems are in comparison to what this Source is able to accomplish. If this power was able to take care of that, surely it's able to take care of whatever it is that I'm concerned about, be it money, business etc.

This is what I want you to get as you think about your desires. Whatever may be going on in your life right now, know that you have support. All you have to do is ask for it. This is why we were given free will. We need to choose and ask for help and stop pushing and fighting our way though the issues.

The Universe knows much more than we do and clearly sees the big picture. The picture and plan that's much greater than we are. There are infinite potential opportunities for the Universe to choose from. Be still for a moment and tune in, you'll see all the different opportunities and solutions to your problems.

Detach and surrender

As you look to fulfill your highest vision, there will come a time when you must learn to trust spirit, let go and surrender. This is a crucial step in the manifestation of your desires. Deepak Chopra writes, "Surrender is faith that the power of Love can accomplish anything even when you cannot foresee the outcome."

I've already shared that letting go is required to make space for something new to come into your life. I want to go further here, and speak more specifically about letting go of your attachments to the manifestation of your dreams to God.

Surrendering and letting go is something many people have trouble with. It takes great strength to surrender and let go. Letting go does not mean giving up. It means that you take your frenetic and anxious energy out of the picture and release your attachment to the outcome. Stop being attached to the form in which your goals and desires will manifest and open yourself to all the different possibilities. Befriend your intuitive guidance system. As the saying goes, "Let go and let God" and get out of the way of the goodness that is coming into your life.

This also goes hand in hand with trusting the Universe. Many times in my own life, I've been forced to trust and let go. It was not something that I consciously chose, but something that God pushed me to do because the very thing I was holding onto was not for my good. Even though at the time it felt like it was and I fought to hold on. As always though, God/Universe knew better and being forced to let go opened up doors for me to receive what was truly best for me.

You may have a strong desire to fulfill a need and make it a reality, however when you're holding it strongly, it oftentimes creates an even greater resistance. When you hold onto it, you begin to attach to the form of how it should come about, versus trusting that whatever you need will indeed be given to you. This is why I love the statement 'this or something better' that is practiced in creative visualization. It acknowledges that you do not know the best version. Our limited mind cannot comprehend the vast abundance and limitless resources and possibilities that are available to us. God/Universe can, so have the strong desire within you, but turn that desire over to the power of the great universe.

Along with letting go is patience. Although it may seem contradictory, patience is an important element to manifesting and living abundantly. I love a line from

A Course in Miracles that states, "Infinite patience creates immediate results." This means being in a state of knowing that all will be taken care of. When you have infinite patience, you are in a relaxed state. You feel aligned and are in the flow with your good and can be confident that your desire is on its way.

Doubt and anxiety create resistance and interrupt the creation process. They add delays to the time it takes for your wish and goals to manifest. With infinite patience, there is no resistance and thus your desires will flow easily and effortlessly to you. The Universe always provides for you, and your life is evolving and growing, as it should.

Faith

To fulfill your greatest desire, you have to have faith that it is possible. Faith is knowing that whatever it is you wish is yours. It's believing that your aspirations are not only possible, but a done deal.

Faith is the knowing that regardless of what is happening around you and the apparent physical lack of your desires that the attainment of it is at hand.

It's believing that the higher power, who through 'all things are possible' is working on your behalf, bringing the right people and conditions to make it a reality. It's trusting that whatever you're currently experiencing is needed to prepare you to receive your dreams.

The conditions you're facing, the resistance and frustrations are there for you to clear in order to receive what you truly want. It's guiding and carrying you to what you aspire to be, have and do.

To have faith is to trust and believe that you can indeed fulfill your dreams, because truly, you're not going to be given anything you don't believe you can have.

I'll give you an example of faith that happened in my life that yielded a big financial miracle for me. When my husband and I were buying our first home together, we had put a down payment on a particular house that the builder delayed extensively. We ended up transferring our down payment into another home from the same builder, as that particular development was already completed and it was a matter of building the house, versus a whole new development like the original one we wanted to buy.

The thing was that this new house was bigger and required more down payment than anticipated, but I thought we would be covered from the down payment from the original house that we had a deposit on.

However, due to credit issues from when I started my business we were forced to come up with a higher down payment than I had originally thought. The worst part was that I got this news just three months prior to when we were supposed to close on our home!

Now, there was money I was supposed to have received from my taxes from the government over a two-year period, however there was a hold on it. This hold went on for two years and I had pretty much given up on the hope that this money would come to me. It was quite substantial as well, due to two-year accumulation. However each time I checked in the past, it was still on

115

hold and no time was given to me for when it was to be released.

So, on the day I received the news from my broker that I needed to come up with quite a bit of money in three months, it was definitely not what I wanted to hear. However, it was quite strange as there was calmness in me at the time. I somehow trusted and had faith that the money would come. Mind you, at that point our business was picking up and I thought to myself, we could possibly see about borrowing some of the money from the business, but it definitely would not cover the full amount needed.

I remember forwarding the email from my broker to my sister and telling her, something in the regard of, 'well here it is. I know all will be well.'

Right after I sent her the email, I said to myself, I am going to call the government again to see. Now I hadn't called them in a while for the money, but something inside of me just felt called and guided me to call again.

Well, I called them and explained to them about the hold, the person I spoke to put me on hold to check the system. When he came back, the next thing out of his mouth shocked me. He said, 'oh the cheque has been released. It was sent to you, and you should receive it this week.' I was in complete shock! Here was something I've been trying to get for two years and just when I received word that I need a huge amount of money, I was told that it was being released to me. I know in my heart of hearts that this was no simple coincidence. It was pure Divine guidance!

I went home that day, rushed to the mailbox and lo and behold, a big cheque was waiting for me. And it was exactly how much money I needed for the rest of the down payment and closing for my home. Literally it was short just by one dollar. I couldn't believe it!

I also believe that the reason why it was held was because the Universe knew what was best for me. Had I received that money earlier when I was asking and begging for it, I would have used it for my business expenses. It would not have been there. God's timing was the perfect timing, exactly when I needed it. Just like God/Universe knew the perfect timing for me to conceive my baby girl!

Your source of supply

I want to pause now and highlight an important truth that changed everything for me. This is about understanding my true source of supply. Hear me on this; your source of supply is not your job, business, customers, partner, investment etc. Although you may receive money from them physically, they are not your source of supply. They are simply different *channels* of your supply.

Your true source of everything, comes from God/ Universe/Spirit; again, insert whatever term fits within your spiritual practice. When you stop focusing on the channels, and rely on your source of supply and see it for what it is; miracles happen.

Focusing on my channels is something I know all to well. I used to own a wellness center, with one of my sisters, and we had different holistic practitioners that worked in our center. I remember always being so nervous and worried when a practitioner chose to leave for whatever reason. I would immediately think that all the clients would leave with them and never come back. I saw the practitioners or rather, the customers as my source of supply.

How many times have you let a job loss, client leaving, or drop in investments affect your sense of supply? Understand that prosperity comes through many forms and channels. It is not limited. When one channel closes, there are many more opportunities of abundance available for you.

Another personal example is that we also had a Corporate Wellness program and one year, our biggest client chose to run their program in-house. This was a big shock and hit to our sales. After the initial disappointment, I went on to acknowledge that that channel was not our supply. Although we made a lot of money through that channel, there was actually a lot of work that came with it. When my sister, who is my business partner, and I really looked at it, it was not aligned to the true vision of how we wanted to work. It forced us to think outside the box and look for opportunities that were more aligned to a business that gave us more freedom, while making the kind of money we wanted to make. Had we continued with that particular contract, we would have remained the same and not grown as much as we did over the years following the end of the contract we had.

The loss of that income made us step outside our comfort zone and as a result were presented with opportunities that were more aligned with the way we wanted to work and live the lifestyle we envisioned. Was it easy? No, there was work involved. It required taking risks that were outside our comfort zone. However, it allowed us to bring to our awareness work that brought us more joy and fulfillment.

When you focus and put all your thoughts on God; your true source of supply and give all your burdens to this supreme power and trust it in the midst of your storms, you'll be supported.

You'll be given opportunities and doors open that give you hope. This hope and faith will keep building to lead you to your path.

As long as you continue to hold on and take the energy off your worry and guilt, you'll be led past the storm and into the calm sea of your desire.

I know this is easier said then done, and your mind will tempt you to quit and do what is 'sensible' and not what our heart calls you to do. The amazing thing is that as long as you think thoughts of abundance and prosperity, you can and *will* fulfill your dreams. The Universe is the source of your abundance and it doesn't care what channel you choose to make more money and be happy. This takes the pressure off having to do something that others think you should do because it gives you the confidence that regardless of what you do, you're able to achieve success and abundance through it.

When you focus on your desire even when circumstances are telling you otherwise, that is true faith, my friend. Faith that leads you to your goals.

Love, joy, great health, abundance are your natural states. All the difficulties you perceive and experience are not natural to this world. The Universe did not create you to suffer. I truly believe that Spirit lives through us and experiences life through us. Remember I said in the first chapter that we have Spirit within us. If this is the case, then Spirit experiences all joy and abundance through you, everyone and me.

Learning to Receive

As you just read, all good and abundance comes from Source. Source uses different channels to bring you your good. Knowing this opens you up to receive in a greater way.

Many times, people reject gifts from others, either because they feel unworthy or guilty taking from them. However, when you realize that these very people are channels that Source chooses to place into your life and deliver your good to you, helps you become a better receiver.

This was something I know all to well. Like many people, I found it much easier to give than receive. I love helping others and being generous, but for some reason I did not like being a receiver. This most definitely may have been a worthiness issue, and one that I learnt a big lesson on after my wedding.

One of my best friends who was living in Europe at the time and one of my bridesmaids wanted to give me money for my wedding. Now because she traveled far and with her family, I refused saying that her being there was enough. She persisted and I just flatly refused the money.

As I look back, I know I felt guilty taking the money from her because a few years back for her wedding, which I had to travel to Italy for, it was at the lowest financial period of my life. My mother-in-law, who happened to be my boyfriend's mom at the time paid for the trip, which I later paid back after things picked up for me. During that time, I had no money to give her for her wedding, which I wanted to, so the thought of her giving me money did not sit right.

Months after my wedding, a close friend of ours came over to my home and pulled out two hundred dollars to give me from my friend. She was now back in Italy and thought this way I would not refuse because I would physically not be able to give it back to her.

I again flatly refused my friend and said no, I did not want it and I'd find a way to give it back to her. I eventually took it because there wasn't a convenient way to give it back, but later I had the biggest 'aha' moment from that experience.

I later realized that God was giving me money through the channel of my beautiful and generous friend, but I kept refusing it. No wonder I had financial struggles at the time. I could have used the money at the time, but I kept rejecting it! My pride and ego got in the way of me receiving a generous gift that was being given to me.

This was sending a strong message to the Universe that I did not want money and refusing abundance (money *and* generosity from my friend) from coming into my life.

More importantly, I was not allowing my friend to feel good about giving to me. The way I loved to give and help those I loved, I was denying my friend the very same privilege to help and give to me.

When I realized this, I made it my mission that whenever someone gave to me, I would graciously accept and be grateful that God was the source of the abundance and using these earth angels to deliver my good to me. To deny them would block my flow, reject my gifts from God, *and* keep those who loved me from assisting me.

This also went beyond monetary needs for me. I've had a hard time asking for things, so I know when I set the intention and work towards my dream, I need to also say YES to all the support and abundance that comes as a result.

Look at your own life as well, and see how many times you've turned down gifts being offered to you, or declining an offer to help you. When you do this, you are rejecting the gifts from the Universe, which are part of the answers to your prayers.

The Power of Prayer

One of the ways to connect to your Source is through prayer. Now many people just on reading the word will automatically think in religious terms. Prayer for me does not have to be associated to any religion, but a way to have direct dialogue and communication with your Creator. It is a powerful practice that has yielded miracles for many and has the power to do the same for you.

You might be wondering, 'well how do I pray?' Do I have to go down on my knees or in an institution? Again, in my opinion, whatever works for you, as long as you feel connected to your Source and have a dialogue with your Creator.

I was watching an episode of Super Soul Sunday on OWN and Iyanla Vanzant, an international motivational speaker and author was on and she shared three of her personal prayers. They were, 'Help!' The second was 'Help me. NOW!' And the third was 'Thank you!' She had others, but according to her these three covered it for her. So you see, it does not require hours at a time kneeling to pray to God, but can be done quickly and short.

When I'm in the need for Divine guidance, I always look to prayer, although it's something I wish I did on a more consistent basis and go straight to right away. I've heard it said that prayer is your asking and it is through meditation that you're able to hear the answers to your prayer. I'm one hundred percent in agreement with this because I believe one must be still and silent in order to hear the loving voice of the Divine.

I also believe in my heart that through regular dialogue with your Higher Power, and again how you define it is up to you, will help you see and move in the direction of your goals and the fulfillment of our dreams. Through prayer you'll be more connected, aligned and able to recognize the happy coincidences that shows up for you, leading you to your dreams.

A powerful way to use prayer for fulfilling your desires is through affirmative prayer. Wikipedia defines affirmative prayer as, 'a form of prayer or a metaphysical technique that is focused on a positive outcome rather than a negative situation.'

What this means is that when praying, instead of focusing on what is wrong and praying to God to relieve what is wrong, you pray for the positive outcome that you want to manifest in your life. So, instead of praying, 'Dear God/Universe, *please* help me find a job', you say

'Thank you God/Universe for my great career that I enjoy, where I get paid doing what I love!' Can you see and feel the difference between the two? One is shadowed with fear, wanting and desperation and the other of gratitude, trust and peace.

If it's a physical aliment that you want to heal, pray for vitality and perfect health and thank your co-creator that it is so!

The true difference between affirmative prayer and traditional prayer is with affirmative prayer you're acknowledging that whatever you're praying about is already happening and coming into your life. As a result, you come from a place of gratitude and joyful anticipation for your good. On the other hand, like I mentioned, many people pray, but yet filled with lack. They are asking for something yet all their thoughts and consciousness are filled with lack and not having, and as a result their vibrational resonance is in wanting, lack and not having it, so they don't receive what they're praying for.

When you know what you want is transpiring, you then become a vibrational match to it. Consequently, you open yourself to receive it into your life.

As it is written in the Bible, "So I tell you, whatever you ask for in prayer, believe that you have received it, and it will be yours." (Mark 11:24).

Footprints in the Sand

I want to end this chapter and book by sharing with you one of my favourite poems I first heard when I was very young. For some reason, the first time I heard this poem, it was as if something truly divine opened up for me. Growing up, I had periods of pain, fear and abandonment, and this poem gave me hope that I was not alone. And in the moments of pain and suffering, I felt like I had someone to help guide me and carry me through. You may already be familiar with this poem, but I'd like to leave you with the words....

Footprints in the Sand

One night a man had a dream. He dreamed He was walking along the beach with the LORD. Across the sky flashed scenes from His life. For each scene He noticed two sets of footprints in the sand. One belonging to Him and the other to the LORD.

When the last scene of His life flashed before Him, he looked back at the footprints in the sand. He noticed that many times along the path of His life there was only one set of footprints. He also noticed that it happened at the very lowest and saddest times of His life.

This really bothered Him and He questioned the LORD about it. LORD you said that once I decided to follow you, you'd walk with me all the way. But I have noticed that during the most troublesome times in my life there is only one set of footprints. I don't understand why when I needed you most you would leave me. The LORD replied, my precious, precious child, I Love you and I would never leave you! During your times of trial and suffering when you see only one set of footprints, it was then that I carried you."

~Unknown

I love this poem because it illustrates how we can feel alone on this path and feel that we've been deserted by this Power. However, it's the exact opposite. This power never leaves us and wants nothing more than our highest good. During our test, this power supplies us and carries us forward, never deserting us in our time of need.

Whatever issues, challenges and obstacles you may be facing, your #1 thing to turn it around is to give it to the loving care of God/Universe. This does not mean to ignore whatever it is you need to do. For instance, if you need to pay your bills, then by all means pay it to the best you can. But DO NOT focus on the fact that you don't have enough to pay all your bills and there's never enough. Just focus on God and the power he has to transform your circumstances quickly and easily.

When you do this, you open the doors for miracles to happen! I know it is easy to read these words but harder to apply when a situation arises that causes you pain and fear. However, most people are programed to worry and focus on the problem versus *trusting* that a solution is at hand. This is the difference between experiencing miracles and staying stuck in your circumstances. You have the choice. Remember free will? You are a thought away to changing your current circumstances to reflect your deepest desires.

You can consciously choose to be divinely guided or allow your old subconscious programming to lead, which subsequently, creates more of the same in the future. Focus on what it is you want to bring into the world and achieve. Focus on service, and contribution and love will emanate from you as you pursue your dreams. That love is your plug to the Universe, the loving Universe that takes care of your every need.

Conclusion

You've now come to the end of your journey with this book, however, the work has just begun. As I stated before, to see results and receive your desires requires you take action on the knowledge and principals laid out in this book. It's through consistent action that you're able to achieve your desires. As you take action towards your goals, the bridge to its fulfillment will appear.

I also want to remind you about the power of integration. Integrate this new way of being into your life. Let it become a habit and something that you do daily so it is a way of being for you. Start using your imagination to constantly see what it is you want to achieve. Let it feel natural and already accomplished. Look to the emotions that you'd feel had it already happen, and live from that place. This is the path and the way to achieve whatever you aspire to and have it become your present reality.

At the end of the day, the core of what you want to fulfill is the connection back to your Source. Every desire of your heart, every aspiration you have is all connected back to Source. Source wants you to live the fullest version of your life. You do not need to gain permission nor do anything to be able to live this life. You can have it all, just by accepting it as your true nature.

Do not speak of your troubles and give energy to

it. Do not speak to your friends, family and colleagues about what is missing from your life. Your goal now is to take your focus on 'aspiring' to the 'fulfillment' of your goals. This is now your work and focus. Only give energy to that which you want to manifest into your life.

Remember, your aspirations and goals must come *through* you and not *to* you. This means it must emerge from within you. It is not outside of you, but must be brought from you. You are the catalyst that brings forth the physical manifestation of your desire. Nothing and I mean nothing outside of you can bring you the peace, love, joy and abundance that you desire. You are the co-creator and as a result the one that needs to hold the vision to bring about your goals.

Communicate your needs and desires to Source through what you hold in your consciousness and the emotions you feel. Who you're *being* and what you hold in your thoughts is being transmitted to Source and will be pictured in your life. It's time to grow and expand into abundance.

I thank you for going on this journey with me and letting me share my message and teaching with you. It is truly an honour to know you hold this book in your hands, trusting me to help you go from aspiring to finally fulfilling your dreams.

Lastly, I want you to have fun as you go through your journey. As you know by now happiness, is your #1 goal, as it will lead you to your dreams.

I believe in you and I love you!

Quotes to Inspire

One of my favourite things to do is read quotes to inspire me. Inspirational quotes are a great way to lift my spirits when I'm experiencing any level of resistance, and also helps to move me into action.

In this section, I've compiled some of my favourite quotes that I've come across over the years. Some of them may be familiar to you and others may not.

I want this book to serve as your companion in your quest to helping you on your journey to your goals. Enjoy the quotes I've compiled and let it ignite the passion and faith in you!

Trust

"We have faith the MOMENT we take a step out into the unknown - even if - and especially if - we are terrified to do it. That is what faith is all about. And consider, that the crazy and unforeseen things that happen in your life are preceding something amazing."
~Mastin Kipp

"The outside world reflects our internal state, and when we shift our perceptions, the world shifts accordingly."
~Gabrielle Bernstein

"I am not what happened to me, I am what I choose to become."
~Carl Jung

"Of all the liars in the world sometimes the worst are our own fears."
~Rudyard Kipling

"Keep your dreams alive. Understand to achieve anything requires faith and belief in yourself, vision, hard work, determination, and dedication. Remember all things are possible for those who believe."
~Gail Devers

"You have all you need within you to become the best version of yourself. Anything that inspires you is an outward reflection of the potential within you. Cultivate in your own life, in your own way, the qualities and greatness you see in others and pretty soon you will be living a life that is your personal version of greatness. Your work is to apply yourself everyday and don't look back."
~Jackson Kiddard

"What could you not accept, if you knew that everything that happens, all events, past, present and to

come, are gently planned by One whose only purpose is your good?"
~A Course in Miracles

"There are only two ways to live your life. One is as though nothing is a miracle. The other is as though everything is a miracle."
~ Albert Einstein

Wealth

"If you believe that you must work hard in order to deserve the money that comes to you, then money cannot come to you unless you do work hard. Financial success, or any other kind of success, does not require hard work. It does require alignment of thought. You simply cannot offer negative thought about things that you desire and then make up for it with action or hard work. When you learn to direct your own thoughts, you will discover the true leverage of Energy alignment."
~Esther Abraham-Hicks

"If all you focus on is money you will have a hard time getting any. Focusing on the money only is like focusing on the apple, but forgetting the seed. The seed of TRUE abundance is not money, but doing what you love. Love is the strongest energy in the Universe and if you step away from the life that you know and begin to step towards a life of doing what you love, you will be planting very powerful seeds. After enough time and care the seeds you plant will begin to blossom and bare amazing

fruit. Money and many other forms of abundance will literally chase you. Focus on what makes you happy, take risks in that direction and don't let anyone tell you it isn't possible. Look to those who inspire you and ask yourself what would they do? These folks know about true abundance, take note."
~Jackson Kiddard

"When I chased after money, I never had enough. When I got my life on purpose and focused on giving of myself and everything that arrived into my life, then I was prosperous."
~Wayne Dyer

"I never focused on the money, I just wanted to help people - and when you help enough people you just can't stop the money".
~Louise Hay

"There are no limitations to the mind except those we acknowledge. Both poverty and riches are the offspring of thought."
~Napoleon Hill

Persistence

"Every great work, every big accomplishment, has been brought into manifestation through holding to the vision, and often just before the big achievement, comes apparent failure and discouragement."
~Florence Scovel Shinn

"It's well known in wisdom communities that delays are not denials. Remember this at all times. Keep focused on what you can do in the moment, and if there is nothing to be done - you are being taught patience. Apply yourself everyday towards your deepest desire - work hard, then let go. This is how mastery is attained."
~Jackson Kiddard

"What you still need to know is this: before a dream is realized, the Soul of the World tests everything that was learned along the way. It does this not because it is evil, but so that we can, in addition to realizing our dreams, master the lessons we've learned as we've moved toward that dream. That's the point at which, as we say in the language of the desert, one 'dies of thirst just when the palm trees have appeared on the horizon. Every search begins with beginner's luck. And every search ends with the victor's being severely tested."
~Paulo Coelho

"When you get into a tight place and everything goes against you, till it seems as though you could not hang on a minute longer, never give up then, for that is just the place and time that the tide will turn."
~Harriet Beecher Stowe

Goals and Dreams

"The key is to listen to your heart and let it carry you in the direction of your dreams. I've learned that it's possible to set your sights high and achieve your dreams

and do it with integrity, character, and love. And each day that you're moving toward your dreams without compromising who you are, you're winning."
~Michael Dell

"All who have accomplished great things have had a great aim, have fixed their gaze on a goal which was high, one which sometimes seemed impossible."
~Orison Swett Marden

"This life has an infinite number of potentials for you; we live in a made to order Universe. Whatever you believe is possible for you and take consistent action upon is what becomes your reality. If you keep telling yourself that your dream isn't possible, you will come to find that you are absolutely right. But my friend, if you draw a line in the sand and tell the Universe that your dreams are a reality RIGHT NOW, and take action as if that were the case, you will come to find that you are absolutely right. The question is how long can you live in the fire of your dreams manifestation?
~Jackson Kiddard

"Start by doing what's necessary; then do what's possible; and suddenly you are doing the impossible."
~St. Francis of Assisi

"I've come to believe that each of us has a personal calling that's as unique as a fingerprint - and that the best way to succeed is to discover what you love and then find a way to offer it to others in the form of service, working

hard, and also allowing the energy of the universe to lead you."
~Oprah Winfrey

"When we create something, we always create it first in a thought form. If we are basically positive in attitude, expecting and envisioning pleasure, satisfaction and happiness, we will attract and create people, situations, and events which conform to our positive expectations."
~Shakti Gawain

"Nothing splendid has ever been achieved except by those who dared believe that something inside of them was superior to circumstances."
~Bruce Barton

"Men often become what they believe themselves to be. If I believe I cannot do something, it makes me incapable of doing it. But when I believe I can, then I acquire the ability to do it even if I didn't have it in the beginning."
~Mahatma Gandhi

"All the concepts about stepping out of your comfort zone mean nothing until you decide that your essential purpose, vision and goals are more important than your self-imposed limitations."
~Robert White

"Where you now stand is a result of thoughts and feelings that you have offered before, but where you are

going is a result of your perspective of where you now stand."
~Esther Hicks

"You were born with potential
You were born with goodness and trust
You were born with ideals and dreams
You were born with greatness
You were born with wings
You are not meant for crawling, so don't
You have wings
Learn to use them and fly!"
~Rumi

Acknowledgements

There are many people who had a major hand in bringing this book into fruition. Some quite literally and others by holding space and encouraging me to share my work and fulfill this dream.

I want to start of by acknowledging my two angels Jaylen and Maleyah. God truly blessed my world by giving me the honour to have you call me mommy. You both push me everyday to be a better person and work to make this world a better place. I'm grateful to have experienced what unconditional love means, by the love that entered my heart at your births.

Then there's my partner in crime, Joel. Thank you for manifesting in my life and co-creating our beautiful family. You teach me more than you'll ever know and I thank you for your commitment to our family and always showing up willing to do whatever it takes to make our family work. I love you and I'm truly grateful for you.

To my incredible mom. I love you and I'm grateful for your love, support and all that you do for my family and me. You've shown me great strength and I am blessed to call you my mom.

And to my amazing sisters, who have been with me through so many highs and lows. I cannot imagine going through some of the darkness in my life without the love and support from the both of you. Your support and love means the world to me and I am incredibly grateful for it.

I want to thank the incredible teachers that have come into my life influencing the way I learn and teach. I am always a student first, and wish to keep on learning so I can become a better teacher. As quoted by Robert A. Heinlein, "when one teaches two learn." As I continue to teach, I learn even more.

There are too many teachers to mention here, but I am grateful that they paved the way for the rest of us to harness their teachings and awaken to our power to create the life of our dreams.

One incredible teacher, mentor and friend that I do want to call out is Michael J. Chase. Thank you for being my friend, and pushing me to share more of me. This was not easy and I had some internal struggles sharing some of the stories, but your words rang in my ears. I cannot thank you enough for your love, trust and belief in my work and me. Your kindness to the world is unmatched.

I have to also thank my wonderful editor Danielle Scruton. I am so happy I went with my gut and entrusted you with my vision for this book. Thank you for loving me enough to be completely honest with my first version. You urged me to go deeper and although difficult to do so, I learnt so much about myself and grew so much through the process. It made this dream of mine better for those who will be touched by it.

A creative genius I need to call out and thank is my beautiful soul sister and graphic designer Tiana Gagic. Thank you for creating this beautiful cover for my book early on, so I can print and have something to visualize and call into existence. Your talent is beyond words and I'm blessed to have you in my life and business.

I also want to thank my incredibly talented friend Joya Williams, who had infinite patience in reviewing my work and providing additional critique and edits. Thank you for being the other eye on my work, making sure it was ready to share and inspire others.

And to my countless friends and colleagues who I've had the pleasure to cross paths with that have met me with so much love and support. Those I've shared great memories with, and sent me love and well wishes as I embarked to complete this book. Your love and support means the world to me, and you will never know how much your comments and well wishes touched my heart.

Last but not least, I thank YOU for reading this book. By picking up this book, no matter how it came into your life gives me great joy and honour. Thank you for reading my words and allowing me the privilege to share my lessons with you, in hopes that it inspires you to reach beyond your wildest dream and have the courage to dare to reach and create the life you've always dreamed of. It is my greatest wish that you know, without a shadow of a doubt, that your greatest aspirations will indeed be fulfilled.

With love and gratitude,
Uchechi

About the Author

Uchechi Ezurike-Bosse is an author, speaker, television host, and entrepreneur. She has created various online and live programs in the field of business and personal development and has been featured as a guest on *Hay House Radio*, a regular contributor to *The Huffington Post*, as well as various online publications.

She's also the author of *Business Success Blueprint ~ A Step-by-Step Process to Creating a Profitable Business You Love*, and the Creator of the *Dream Life Designer Planners*.

Uchechi is also the proud Community Producer and Host of *Empowered Living in Durham Region*, which airs on Rogers TV in a Canadian Community.

She's been dubbed the 'Dream Whisperer' by clients

and is passionate about educating and empowering others to cultivate the right conditions to effortlessly manifest their dreams, so they can live the highest vision for their lives.

She lives in a town east of Toronto, Canada with her loving husband and beautiful son and daughter whom she credits for inspiring and pushing her to be her very best.

For more information about Uchechi Ezurike-Bosse and her work, please visit her at www.myempoweredliving.com.

CPSIA information can be obtained
at www.ICGtesting.com
Printed in the USA
LVOW08s0613310117
522664LV00001B/13/P